Dreams and Nightmares of a Menopausal Woman

By Bambi Davis

Gotham Books

30 N Gould St.
Ste. 20820, Sheridan, WY 82801
https://gothambooksinc.com/

Phone: 1 (307) 464-7800

© 2023 *Bambi Davis*. All rights reserved.

No part of this book may be reproduced, stored in a retrieval system, or transmitted by any means without the written permission of the author.

Published by Gotham Books (November 1, 2023)

ISBN: 979-8-88775-618-9 (P)
ISBN: 979-8-88775-619-6 (E)

Because of the dynamic nature of the Internet, any web addresses or links contained in this book may have changed since publication and may no longer be valid.

The views expressed in this work are solely those of the author and do not necessarily reflect the views of the publisher, and the publisher hereby disclaims any responsibility for them.

Table of Contents

Foreword v

Volume 1 1

Volume 2 21

Volume 3 56

Volume 4 86

Volume 5 118

Bambi Davis has also authored a preschool children's book titled, <u>**"BRUSH"**</u>. The adventures of Bella learning about different brushes and the many uses for the word-**"BRUSH"**.

Coming Soon

<u>**"Rice Belly"**</u> William Chandler lays in a hospital bed when the Japanese conquer the island, in WWII. William becomes a prisoner of war. A collection of actual letters to his wife, while imprisoned.

<u>**"Rice Belly II"**</u> William Chandler, Japanese prisoner of war, didn't just write to his wife. A collection of actual letters to his father, while imprisoned.

<u>**"My Perfect Horse"**</u> A coloring book that is more than just a coloring book. "My Perfect Horse" is a counting book, 1-10, with a story written in rhyming syllabic verse.

FOREWORD

This book is composed of <u>actual</u> dreams and nightmares. I have epilepsy caused by hormones, or pharmaceuticals. During menopause, my own body's hormones caused me to have grand maul seizures. What makes this book unique is that the rare occurrence of being allergic to my own body occurred, making my brain extremely active. Every time I shut my eyes to sleep I would have a dream or nightmare. I dream in full color. My dreams are so real, to me. I often speak or cry, out loud, during a dream.

During this time I was able to record five legal pads of dreams and nightmares, in great detail. They appear here as written in my dream journal, no added fluff or description. Many of these dreams are hilarious, many are terrifying, and some are sexual.

The names of some people, mostly family members, have been changed for their privacy. Names of celebrities have been retained.

There are times when I am upset with my husband-in my dreams. Rest assured there are no problems with our relationship. We are very much in love and have been together for 37 years. There was no reason for me to feel upset with my husband, at any time. He is quite devoted to me and me to him.

References to Puppa, or Puppa Chubba, are about my, Chihuahua, service dog. He rarely left my side and was greatly bonded to me. Puppa helped me with my seizures, and other medical problems, for 13 1/2 years. I rescued him at the age of 1 1/2; he died at the age of 15. I still mourn his passing.

Native Americans believe that each person has nine animals that make up their characteristic. This is called a person's animal totem- the dragonfly is part of my totem:

"Dragonfly medicine is of the dreamtime and the illusionary facade we accept as physical reality. Dragonflies shifting of color, energy, form and movement explode into the mind of the observer bringing vague memories of a time or place where magic reigned.

Some legends say that dragonfly was once Dragon and that Dragon had scales like dragonflies wings. Dragon is full of wisdom, and flew through the night, bringing light on its fiery breath. The breath of Dragon brought forth the art of magic and illusion of changing form. Dragonfly is the essence of the winds of change. If you feel the need for change, call on dragonfly to guide you through the myth of illusion to the pathway of transformation."(Medicine Cards Sams & Carson, Bear & CO)

This book is intended for entertainment purposes only, enjoy.

VOLUME 1

January 13

I was in a house full of family members. They were so many of them. I tried to work but their noise disturbed me. I got mad. Dad, Mom, I and someone else, (unknown), got into Dad's truck. We drove to pick up people for their 50th anniversary party. Mom and I were in the back of the truck. Mom looked lovely, all in white, and with four corsages. We picked up a Mrs. Maxfield, someone I never met. I stated to everyone that the party was yesterday. Mrs. Maxfield and Mom started to cry. We drove through Sunapee heading to Newport. While going through Sunapee we saw a Native American girl sitting on the grass with some fellows. She had 2 eagle feathers in her hair; the feathers were located on the right side of her jaw. I thought she was my daughter so we stopped. I approached the girl to find out she was not my daughter. Some Native American men were there and they recognized me. One of them came with us in the truck. We were driving to Newport and the road became a river. Very much like the Merrimack, only cleaner and more rapid. Dad's truck had no problem putting up the river (rather James Bond-ish). We went through rapids and were making good progress. I started to notice a lot of beer and soda cans at the bottom of the river. These were from a road repair crew. The cans bothered me greatly. Someone noticed on the left side of the river bank a stack of money. Dad drove close to the money and someone leaned out of the truck and grabbed the stack of bills. On the same side of the river bank there was a pile of old coins. Dad jumped out of the truck, he was driving, and started picking up the coins. With no driver in the truck we started to wash down the river. We swirled and started hitting rocks. We wash down the river quickly hitting things as we went. We got into a city much like Manchester with lots of brick buildings. We started smashing into cars and buildings, so the truck was getting damaged. The truck got hung up on a building and I climbed over people into the driver's seat. The truck was stalled and I had a hard time starting it. I pushed in the clutch and shifted into gear. I found the clutch to be almost gone and the shifter had to be held into place, because it wouldn't stay there. It was a battle to get going again, up the river. We were almost back to the point where Dad jumped out for the coins when I awoke.

January 15 - Afternoon Nap

My husband, my dog and I went for a walk. Along the walk we came across a one-room little house. We went inside. There was a military related room inside with carpet, a couch, a desk with a chair and posters on the wall. When we left the house, we were in another time. The room/house was like a time capsule. My son was there, as a two or three-year-old child (he is now 32). We walked along the river's edge, the water was black. The ground was also black making the river and land hard to determine which was which. My son began to cry as we started back. Near the little building were many military men in dark blue uniforms. Some were in boats giving tours to civilians. Some were doing flips into the water from a high barrack across the river bank. I was very tired and needed to rest. My husband sat down, I laid my head in his lap and cuddled my son. An officer came by and started to visit with my husband. He was very nice young and handsome. The officer said he was headed to

Seattle and it would take six more trips to get there. I, being tired, said "Seattle, Washington"? The man laughed at me, thinking me stupid and replied; "Is there any other"? My husband, my son and I walked a little ways away from the military men. Our old bull mastiff, Eli was there. Chris was so happy to see his dog. They ran and played together. After a while my husband and I went to the little house to go home. Inside the little house was the officer sitting on the couch. There was a big puddle of dog pee in the corner. My husband and I saw the mess and were disgusted. We told the officer our dog didn't do that mess. He was nice and kind and said he knew. I awoke feeling good to see my son as a baby and my old dog Eli.

January 17

My husband and I lived where we do now but we had another house behind this one. The other house was older. I started moving things into the older house. We were going to move into the older house and remove the house in front. One day as I was bringing stuff to the old house I found Dr. Sullivan's wife and children in our house. The doctor had removed walls, pulled up floors and carpets. He had busted my belongings including something that belonged to my grandmother. He basically destroyed our home. I started screaming at him room by room. I was in a mad frenzy. He busted sinks and totally destroyed the house. He thought the home had belonged to him and his family. He was so wrong. I informed him and his family that the house was not his and that he needed to fix or replace everything. As I was going to get my husband, to open a can of whoop ass, I awoke.

January 27

My family, including my son, rented a large home. We were only in the home for a week when a whole troop of snobby upper-class people came into the home. They were there to judge my housekeeping skills. The living room was a mess due to Legos all over the place. The snobs were white gloving everything. They wanted to throw us out, after only a week. I went next door to get my son and he wouldn't come home to clean up his mess. I was walking back to our rental with a cup of neon tetra fish and crying. I stumbled and the fish flew out of the cup into the snow. I started to scream "No", but no sound would come out. I screamed over and over but still nothing came out. Next thing I was climbing the stairs into the home, all the critics were watching me climb the stairs crying, I awoke.

January 30

I don't know where I was, for some reason, I think Colorado even though I've never been there. I was alone and walked into a city. When I got there I saw a man who had sexually molested a four year old girl. He didn't see me. I crept up behind him and took his pistol from his holster. It was in a nicely tooled leather holster. He quickly turned around. I had the pistol drawn on him. I took a full magazine from him, which was also in his holster. I don't know if I shot him or not (I should've). I went running out of the city and down the side of the road. I noticed I was leaving tracks. So I took a pitchfork from somewhere. I started using the pitchfork as a pole vault. Now my tracks were just close circles every 10 feet or so I was making good distance and time. A river ran beside the road, (kind of like the river along Route 114 in Grantham). I saw some people walking on the road up ahead. So I took to the river. It wasn't deep so I kept on pole vaulting up the river. Further up the river I noticed several pair of blue jeans thrown onto the river bank. I stopped to investigate; the pockets were full of money. I took the money from two pair of jeans and started pole vaulting up the river again. I awoke.

February 2

I did not dream of being pregnant. My husband and I had a baby. It was ugly and had a chicken neck, long and thin. (I can't have children due to a hysterectomy in real life). I felt having the child was a nuisance. Outside our apartment building (we own a home in real life), people were gathered. These people were trying to stop moose hunting season. They were protesting to save the moose. I went out to explain that without hunting, many moose would die of starvation. I also explained that many moose would take to the roads during the winter and many people would die from crashing into them. Moose hunting would in fact save the moose and people (no anger was involved). I awoke.

February 14

A woman and her adult son moved into our house. My husband went away for a few days. During that time, the woman started packing up my stuff and putting all my things into the basement. She was moving me out. I called the police and they sided with her.

I tried to explain that I had lived here for 20 years and that it was my house. I awoke.

March 31

I awoke at 6:30 AM. I don't know why. I fell back asleep my husband woke me up a little while after seven, saying I was crying in my sleep. I don't know what the dream was about. I recall that each stride in my dream was huge, catching lots of air as I ran.

April 13

My husband and I bought a new home close to an older home. The house had wood floors and my brother, B, was visiting. One night, I woke up to see there in my bedroom was a little green leprechaun getting under the floorboards. I jumped out of bed and grabbed him. I hollered to my husband and brother who were shocked at what I had hold of. We continued to peel back the floorboards. We found his cache. Under the boards was a pit walled in by boards. In the pit was candy soup! A soup made of deep beautiful honey and candy. It wasn't in buckets or containers. We let the leprechaun go and told him he could keep his cache. We boarded it back up. For some reason, we all slept on the floor near the cache that night; the three of us in a row, sleeping. The next day my brother came to see me. He explained that he knew how the leprechaun kept his candy soup. He had a wooden square in his hands. When he held the edges of the square, the middle would accordion down like a bowl, nice, neat, and watertight. I awoke.

April 18

My husband, my dog, Puppa and I went for a ride in a pickup truck. My husband had a cinnamon Doberman pinscher with him. We pulled over beside the road. My husband claimed that the Doberman could drive the truck! Puppa and I went into the back bed of the truck. The dobby got in the driver's seat and my husband got into the passenger seat. The Doberman put the truck into gear and gunned it. The truck was in reverse! We went over bridge and landed in a river. As we landed in the river my husband woke me because I was whimpering and crying in my sleep again.

April 25

My husband, I, and a friend, Lisa, were traveling together. We were tired and stopped at a house to rest. The house was a rest stop, always open. A young boy let us in the house. We were allowed rest and free clothes. I was so tired that every few step I took I fell down. I was constantly falling down. This concerned my friend Lisa- who had, in real life, a brain aneurysm. After resting, we went into a room full of clothes. Lisa and I found some cute clothes and put them on. I awoke when my daughter called at 1 AM.

May 4

Things were terrible! My husband and I, for some reason, had to go live with Michelle. I had a bedroom very much like a tent; my husband was in the main house. I lay down in my quarters to sleep. Terribly uncomfortable, I picked up a book to read. A winged bug came out of the book. The bug crawled onto my bed and had a baby bug. The baby was white and ready for life upon birth. I looked around and there were many bugs. I was freaked out. I started turning the pages of the book and found the bug had eaten out the whole inside the book. I dropped the book and jumped out of bed. I looked down at the bed and there were many small sticks coming up through the bed. They'd been cut off into points. No wonder I couldn't sleep, being jabbed by the sticks. I decided to get dressed to go out to the main house. My clothes were full of bugs! I Found a towel and put that around myself and went to the main house. My husband and Michelle's son, John, were there. My husband and I had an argument when I complained about my sleeping quarters. My husband got really mad and slammed out of the house. I sat on the stairway to cry. My towel fell away and my old sagging body was exposed! John saw me naked! I apologize to John, crying. I decided to leave my husband and the living conditions. An old friend from school, Rochelle, appeared. She said "do you know me? I'm your old friend, Rochelle"? I looked at her and said, "who cares" and walked out into the night crying. A bunch of heavy equipment, dump trucks, trailers, bulldozers etc. were making a road in our backyard to get to the property next door. They were going to build a house there. The easiest access was through our property. I was screaming at the truck operators; "You don't have permission to make a road through our property!" They didn't care. I awoke.

May 20

I heard a woman cry and knew it was my daughter's soul. At first I couldn't tell if it was my daughter or granddaughter's soul. I know, now, that it was my daughter's soul. I awoke.

June 9

I was near some river. There, I saw my husband with an ex-girlfriend. I was pissed off. I ran up to them and grabbed the other woman. I threw her, headfirst into the river. My husband was pissed at me and told me he didn't want to be with me anymore. I told him fine and I want the house. He agreed to the trade-off. I awoke.

August 6

My husband and I bought a post and beam cabin by a lake. We moved in with our granddaughter. One day the lake receded quite a bit and I thought that was so odd. I saw our ferret and it ran into our house. I ran into the house after it. It ran up the wall and under a beam. The beam was loose. I didn't know about the loose beam until the ferret moved it. My breasts hurt so I lifted up one see what was wrong. I was freaked out! My breasts looked like an alien mouth with teeth! It was feeding on my body! Great purple wounds were on my body under my breasts.

My dream switched:

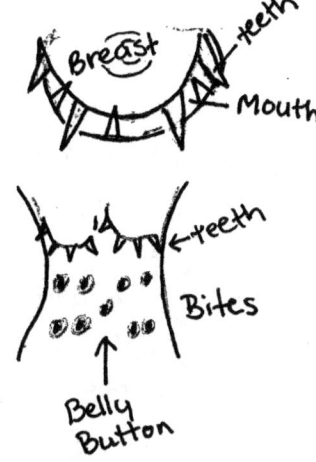

Next a rat sized thing came out from the floor! I stepped on it to stop it. I grabbed a board and started beating its skull in! I pulverized its head! Another rodent came out of the floor; it was the size of a pit-bull! It jumped onto my lap! I started screaming for my husband. I started beating it with the board! The other littler rodent came back to life! I was beating them both and screaming for my husband. Then my husband woke me up.

August 25 – Demerol Dream

My friend, Suzie and I were in the city (could have been Manchester's lower end). We were in my little red Ford Escort, riding around. We were driving by some open shed- type buildings and I spotted a large cage of monkeys. We got out of the car to investigate. There were lots of animals in the sheds; monkeys, apes, zebras and an elephant. We were wondering if a circus was around. While looking around I noticed a plowed up plot of ground about a quarter to a half mile away. Suddenly, lots of granules started spraying over the plowed up plot. The granules were spraying in waves. Suzie and I could feel the granules starting to hit us. The granules stung. We felt something was terribly wrong. All the animals started to panic. Suzie and I started going back to the car. I looked at Suzie; she had purple fluid coming out of her tear ducts. She looked at me and saw the same purple fluid coming out of mine. My shoes had turned a strange color of orange. We quickly looked around and saw most of the animals were dead! Then we noticed a vat- type container. The vat had a hole in the side of it and a little blonde girl, about five years old, peeked out. She was looking scared with purple fluid seeping out of her tear ducts. We yelled to her to come with us. She quickly scampered out of the vat and we all headed toward my car. On the way to my car we saw elephant trunks lying on the ground between the spaces in large crates. Everything had died around us. We got in the car and sped away. Ahead, I saw military men with gas masks and machine guns; they had put up a roadblock. I whip the car around and went another way. There was another roadblock. Military men were everywhere. I finally decided to take the path of least resistance and chose to go through the roadblock that consisted of only three military men. I figured that if I was as close as possible to them, they would have a less chance of hitting us. Maybe if they felt they'd get hit by my car, they wouldn't be able to shoot so well. I gun the car. We were going for it! Just as I was about to run them down and they were raising their guns,- shots rang out. Someone behind the military guys shot the soldiers to allow us to escape. All three soldiers just fell over as we were about to go by them. Speeding off, with purple stuff streaming down our faces, the little girl told us what direction we should take. I was so freaked out over everything going on. It was easy for me to just follow the girl's directions. We arrived at a river. There were many people on horseback traveling up the stream. The little girl told us, softly, to jump in and swim downstream. We jumped in. The water was clear and rinsed the purple off our faces. I could see skulls on the rocky river bottom. As we swam slowly downstream, we passed many people, all going upstream. A couple of people had stopped with their horses. One of the horses had ripped out his frog! (1) It was in such pain and probably, dying. We continued downstream. An old lady spoke to us as we passed. She was in such a get-up. She sat on a throne type seat upon her white horse. There was a piece framework around her and the horse. Mosquito netting covered her and most of the horse. This looked so odd, all white and ritzy, with purple juice flowing from her and the horse's eyes. She said "don't go that way, there is nothing there ". We continued on downstream. As we neared a park looking area, quite a ways downstream, the little blonde girl told us we should get out of the water there. I don't know why we trusted and listen to the little girl. She seemed to know things. It all seems familiar to me. Then it clicked, like in *Stephen King's "Stand"*, people being guided by someone, mentally, to safe haven. We got out of the river and followed a concrete pathway. It spiraled down into the earth and became like a bar/amphitheater.

Nobody was alive there. A few dead people were slumped at the bar with purple juice stained faces. We continued to the back room. In the room was an old fountain. The little girl asked me to rip it apart. Layer by layer, I ripped the stone away. I dismantled the fountain to the floor. People started showing up. I kept going, below the floor, to reach the fountain source. Many people had plastic jugs with them. I was concerned because we had no jugs. The little blonde girl said it was all right. We had all been called, and we all had a part. The young men who had shot soldiers stepped forward with a smile. The people with the jugs said they had enough for all of us. Finally, I arrived at the fountain source, very deep below the floor. I woke.

1   Frog: a very tender part, in the center, of a horse's hoof.

August 26

I awoke, one early winter day, to the sound of a couple of male kids goofing around in our side yard, along Fortune Lane. I shined a flashlight out of the window and hollered for them to get out of here; "Get off our property!" Next, I noticed a herd of sheep on Fortune Lane making a raucous. A gold and brown Camaro was herding them around. The car herded them onto Old Post Road. The driver got them nicely spread out from our front yard to the corner. He then got a running start and plowed right through the whole sheep herd. The sheep, literally, exploded upon impact! I was mortified! I knew the sheep belonged to the neighbors up Fortune Lane. I went outside and up Fortune Lane to tell the neighbors about their sheep being killed. The neighbor and a young woman, probably her daughter, were sitting out on the side of the road. They asked if we had had any neighbor trouble. I replied "no". The neighbor and her daughter started walking down to our house with me, while I was telling them about their sheep herd. On the side of our property, abutting Fortune Lane, there was a bunch of rotting junk that was out for a yard sale. I was appalled by the crappy old junk on our property. There was a rotted out old cook stove, old rotted out kitchen master combo breadbox, and some photo albums (all crap). I hollered "who dumped their junk on our property"? The neighbor exclaimed, "It is no longer your property". The town had taken 65 feet of our property along Fortune Lane. There were large bear tracks in the dusting of snow around the junk pile. The neighbors, themselves, had taken advantage of our loss and had set up the yard sale. These neighbors then showed up. They had been down Old Post Road getting two of their bear dogs. The dogs were in cages in the back of his truck. He was smiling and happy to have his dogs back. My husband came out of the house to see what the ruckus was about. The neighbor told my husband that we would have to come up with some money quick or have his legs broken! My husband glared back, "what for?" The neighbor said "if you want to have your property back you have to pay for it". We looked up along our property line and the town had winged back with the snow plow 65' all along our Fortune Lane property line. A funny drain was put in where our perimeter drain came out. The neighbor stated "good thing you had water coming from that drain constantly; otherwise, the town would've wiped out our drain as well". I awoke.

August 28

I was working at Market Basket! There were two large dog craps in the aisle. My job was to count pastries. It was a hot day and the pastries were melting. The job was frustrating and I couldn't keep proper inventory. The end.

August 30

I was living in a small trailer with my boyfriend (Kiefer Sutherland or some Baldwin brother, some rough guy). He got into an argument with some other guy. Things were getting violent quickly. He reached out and grabbed me by the head! I put both my arms up over my head to protect myself. I hollered "It's me! Please stop". He snapped out of it and set me down. I awoke.

August 31

I got a job at a supermarket. The market was a celebrity supermarket. Kevin Bacon worked in the meat department. I Dream of Jeannie worked in the candy/ cookie aisle. Each isle department had a different celebrity working in it. Sylvester Stallone was there. It was great. Only well-known celebrities worked there. Not saying I was a celebrity. People could work with them on a temporary basis or just see them while shopping.

November 6

A heavyset girl, with green eyes and brown hair (the top layer of her hair was black), asked me if I wanted to take a trip with her. I said "sure", and we went on a train. We went to Prague. We walked down walkways, looking around. I met Ben Affleck and we flirted. (Weird)! I had to go back home. The girl decided to go back to Prague. I said I'd go with her. We got on the train again. Puppa

Chubba, my dog, showed up. He had followed me. I was concerned because I didn't have a leash with me. We walked the walkways again. We went down some stairs. My dog started to take a crap halfway down the stairs. I yelled at him and ran down the stairs. When I got to my dog I saw that the stairs were covered in dog crap. So I just let Puppa finishes his business. The girl and I stepped over the poops. I awoke.

November 10

I was at my friend Jill's. Her home was in a complex, very dorm room like. She had six or so rooms. On that day, I was there but Jill was not. A group of men, about five, came bursting into her apartment. The men started taking her bed apart and walked out with it. I started yelling at them, "Stop! Jill needs her bed. What do you think you're doing? No!" The men didn't care. Each one took a piece out and was gone in a flash. I was crying, thinking what will Jill do without her bed? After crying for a while I started to roam her apartment. All the doors, to each room, were shut. I opened each door to look in each room. In each room, I found at least one or more beds. I knew there were only three people in Jill's family, but found so many beds. I stopped worrying about the one bed that had been taken. Then I started wondering why she had so many beds. I awoke.

November 13

Michael Jackson made me into a geisha girl. Ha, ha. He did a beautiful job of my makeup. I looked lovely. After making me a geisha, we danced to slow music at some gathering. I felt honored and beautiful. I awoke.

November 14

I owned a discount store here in Newbury. It was raining and there were leaks at the edges of the wall. Puppa, my dog, had peed in a few spots and I was walking around to see where he might have peed. I kept hearing the water drip. My store was only half the building; I walked into the other half, which was a garage. It was leaking badly in there. John D. was there. I said, "Hi". He wanted to know if I had anything sweet to eat in my store. I said, "Sure do". We walked around the store and I pointed out many sweet items, and said, "help yourself". A few customers came in. I was the only employee and was having trouble taking care of people at the register. A woman came in and wanted to know where she could get a hot bowl of cream of chicken soup. I suggested Four Corners Grill. I woke.

November 19

My husband owned the Springfield store. It still had all the beautiful old oak mailboxes in it. The problem was the place was filthy! There were crumbs, dust and clutter all over the place. I spent all night cleaning his store and those dusty mailboxes. The End.

November 21

My Grammy passed away years ago; she had a beaver problem at her house. She wanted my husband and me to come and take care of the problem. When we got there the water was up so high you couldn't get through the front door. We had to wade a bit to get into the side door. From the road we could see a swirling hole of water, then the dam. Another swirling hole told us where the beavers' home was, it was bank beavers. Most of the property was underwater. My husband and I went into the house, which was a mess. The foundation was collapsing; none of the floors were level. The bedroom, I used to sleep in, was shaped like a bowl- high on the sides and low in the middle. Every room was full of garbage and clothes. It was gross! My husband asked why things were so bad and I said, "She's old, on Social Security and fat. She can't take care anymore". I went out to look at the barn. There were lots of oatmeal boxes out there. The barn was coated with manure and straw. Our old cat was in the barn. He came to me and was covered with manure and straw. You couldn't tell he was a black and white cat. He looked like a shitty straw porcupine. I awoke

END OF VOLUME 1

VOLUME 2

December 28

My husband and I were living at my parent's house. Should I say at the location where their house used to be. A large old wooden three-story house was where their house used to be. My husband had ridden his motorcycle to Grantham, he was mad at me and going to see a girlfriend. When my husband came back he was on a skateboard. My son, Hayman, Jim and his girlfriend came over to visit. We were all standing outside visiting. Hayman noticed a lot of bubbles coming up out of the river down back. He asked if there was any volcanic activity going on. We watched the bubbles increase and moved forward toward the back bank, closest to the house. All of a sudden a large green dinosaur came out of the water! We all went into the house to hide. The dinosaur smashed in through the windows and doors. Hayman and Jim were eaten. My son, I and Jim's girlfriend ran for an interior closet. A little dinosaur chewed through into our hiding place. I grabbed it and held on. When the big dinosaur tried to get us in the closet I threw the little dinosaur at the big one. The big one ate the little one. At that point we ran upstairs. The dinosaurs were still crashing through the windows! I kicked a little dinosaur in to the path of the big dinosaur, which immediately munched him. My son was scared. Hell, we all were. We went to the third floor of the house and went into a closet. In the closet around the corner was another closet, deep within the house. I don't know what happened to my husband. It was just my son, a girl and I hiding there. We stayed there until there was no more noise. The dinosaur moved on and we were safe. I awoke.

January 1

We lived here on this property but our house was a lot older. There was a porch like on the old house that burned. The porch was out back similar to where our sliding door is now. A sow bear and her three cubs, came onto the porch. Her cubs were no larger than my Chihuahua, Puppa Chubba. I took a broom and shooed her off the porch. I picked up her cubs and put them out. There was another sow with cubs outside. Our backyard was full of black bears. When I came back into the porch I noticed that Puppa Chubba was not in the house. He was out with the bear cubs. I panicked. I awoke.

January 2

It was my birthday. I received a helicopter as a gift. I got in the pilot seat; my son and husband were with me. I couldn't get it off the ground. But I could move it forward. So we went for a ride down the road. We were maybe a half an inch off the ground. I wanted to go higher but couldn't. There were all kinds of people flying above the road. Some had flying shoes. Some had jet packs. Some people had helicopters. The flying traffic was heavy. I was below everyone and was afraid of hurting someone if I lifted off higher. I awoke.

January 3

I was walking in a small city area and came across a secondhand shop. The shop was having a lottery. For $100 you can get a chance to look around the store to find the one special item that would be the winner. The winner won the building. The building was old and not in the best of shape. So, I took a chance. I rummaged around the shop; there were clothes, collectibles and jewelry. I'm not into jewelry but I decided to look through it. There was a tall green bureau with little drawers. Each drawer had jewelry in it. I looked it over and chose the bottom drawer to start my search. There were a couple of other women in the store; they were looking through the clothes for the winning item. I opened the bottom drawer and started pouring through the items. A necklace, nondescript, had a piece of paper attached to it in the paper said "Winner! I shouted, jumped up and ran to the counter with it. I had won the building! The woman at the counter closed the store then gave me a tour of the building. The building was her home. There was room upon room. In the old wooden house one room was so bad the floor was V-shaped. That room was like in the little house in the White Mountains at Clark's trading post I went to tell my husband about my winning. I awoke.

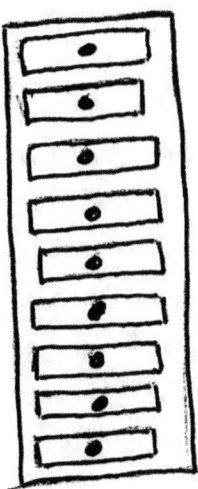

January 3

My husband joined a triathlon type race. I think they were more than three parts to the race. My friend Sue was with me at the race. My husband did well in the first part. When it came to the swimming part, my husband didn't want to do it. He wanted to quit, he was tired. I was surprised that he wanted to quit, I was a little upset over it. I turned around and walked away, my friend came with me. We walked into a shop near the lake. It turned out to be a candy shop. Oh joy! Nobody but us was there. We started sampling the goods. There were caramels, jellies, Mints, and chocolates. We ate all we could. I awoke.

January 10

My husband, granddaughter and I lived in an apartment. Things were not so good. One day I took a train to another town. The train was so strange with many stories, levels. The berths were like studio apartments. We were going to a farm we had bought. My granddaughter and I were on a lower level of the train. We had to go up three flights of stairs to get off the train. While riding in our studio apartment berth my husband showed up. He was surprised we were there. And we were surprised he was there. I asked him where he was going. He said, "To town to buy a bed". I asked him, "why"? He said, " I've been having a relationship with another woman. I need another bed for our home, so we don't sleep together". I wasn't bothered by this and replied," save your money, just go to your girlfriend's house to have sex and sleep there on those nights. Then on nights you're not having sex with her come home and sleep in your own bed, as long as you don't have sex with me." My husband agreed with this. We turned and notice that our granddaughter was gone! We went searching for her. My husband found her three flights up. Our granddaughter was only a toddler in my dream and I was freaked out about her stair climb! There were no rails on the stairs. The stairs were like spiral stairs with one side attached to the wall. I thanked my husband and got off the train, leaving him behind. My granddaughter and I went to the farm we had bought. It was wonderful. Just as when we bought it. I put my granddaughter down for nap and then when outdoors. I walked around the yard. In the front field/yard I made a startling discovery. Many rocks had been removed from the property. Where the rocks had previously been, there were deep pits with water in the bottom of each one. The water in the bottom of the holes worked like a tide. The water receded and then came back in a rhythm. The pits were deep like lake wells. I was very upset; this was very dangerous for my granddaughter. I hadn't noticed the missing rocks due to a fence, made out of little strips of wood very much like Popsicle sticks. A retaining wall had been backfilled. There were three small birch trees that were half buried. I went to the farm across the way to ask about the missing rocks and the retaining wall situations. The farmer's wife came to the door when I knocked. They had a big beautiful farm, very fancy. When I asked the wife about the stones she replied," Oh yes my husband did that". I replied, "well- that was on my property." She said, "No -it was on our land". And that the retaining wall was our property line. I replied," no", pointing at the low concrete stone wall at our feet.

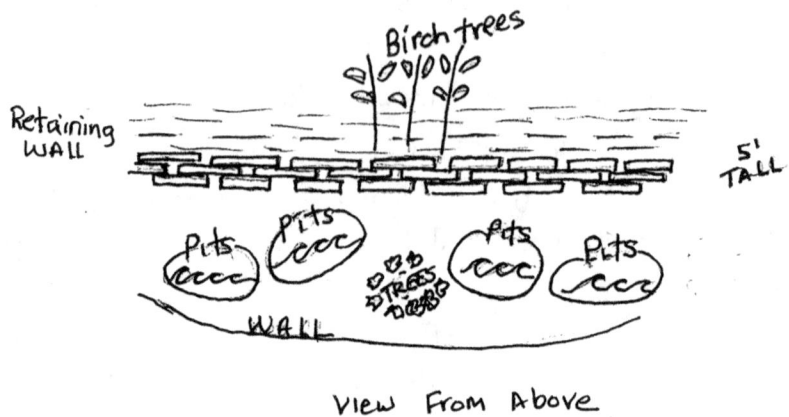

View From Above

This is your property line." She gasped and explain, Holy cow! You're right. Then I told the woman about my granddaughter, and the danger the rock removal could cause. The farm's wife went into her house to speak to the farmer. He was an old grump, but agreed to pay for the rocks. I went to the pits without the rocks at once and began pushing the dirt into the holes. Then I noticed the birch trees half buried. I went back across the street to that farm to talk to the farmer's wife again. I explained that burying my birch trees was going to kill them. Then they questioned whether I had a toddler or not. I went home and got my granddaughter up from her nap. We went outside to prove her existence. The farmer and wife thought she was beautiful and precious. The farmer paid extra for killing the birch trees. I had to fill in the holes by hand and remove the retaining wall. I awoke.

January 14

We were living at mom and dad's in Springfield. A group of us were outdoors in the field. I have no idea who was with us. I know that Puppa Chubba and I were there. We were all visiting when all of a sudden a large red bovine came crashing through the woods, into the brook and then into the field. I was scared for Puppa! The bovine was stampeding right towards him. I screamed and ran towards Puppa and scooped him up, just in time. The bovine stopped right in front of us. I patted and scratched the cows' head. It was short but huge. As we, wandered around and visited, the bovine followed us around. We went into the house. The cow came in also. I tried to get the red cow out, but it wouldn't go. There was a blanket on the floor behind the couch, the bovine went to the blanket and lay down on its side. I went over to look him over. I looked at its legs and saw that they were very short. I looked at its head and moved the hair from its eyes and saw they were very small. I'd not seen any dairy or beef cow like this. I came to the conclusion that this was Buffalo. I asked, "Are you a Buffalo"? The bovine replied, "Yes I am". He was gentle and very tired. We spoke to each other for a little while, then he napped and I awoke.

January 23

I worked at a bank in Newport. It was located were the old Ben Franklin store was, where a gym is located today. It seemed to be in the 1950s. My coworkers were all women. I'd come into some money, legally, maybe a lottery. I bought a beautiful house on 35 acres. I had a party and invited all my coworkers from WPI factory. This was odd because I worked with them in 1999. I didn't tell anyone at my bank job about the winning s or the new house. Cheryl, my friend, came to my party. She sat in a chair in the living room. She was hungry so I made her some food. She sat in the chair all night. Some of my party guests swam in my indoor pool. Some spent the night in my many bedrooms. The next day when the party was over and everyone had left I noticed that the upholstery in the chair that Cheryl had sat in was worn out; there were holes where her butt had been. I got into a new green pickup truck. It was a beautiful 1950s pickup truck that had awesome rounded fenders. I drove to pick up a coworker and we went to work. As we drove I told her about buying the house and getting the money. She didn't believe me until we got out of the truck and she took a look at it. There was a line of men waiting to get into the bank, when we arrived. When I got out of the truck I was topless!! The men were shocked that I was bare breasted. My body was as poor as it is today – nothing perky or sweet. I had all the tattoos that I have today. As I walked past the men in line, one of the men, (all rednecks) had tattoos. The tattoos were awful prison type, home done ink. I mentioned that his tattoos were crap, and showed him mine. I didn't show my prizewinner on my right thigh, but I tried to tell him about it. I had trouble talking. My voice was only a whisper. I tried to speak louder but it just wasn't coming out. I went back to my beautiful green truck and put on a shirt. The men saw my truck and were upset, jealous, I think. I went into the bank and was talking with my coworkers. One of the girls looked out the window and told me the men were messing with my truck. I quickly went outside to stop the vandalism. A couple of the men had the passenger side back tire off and were messing with my brakes. Two men were watching what was going on. The man closest to me had a rifle; he was not holding it tightly. I grabbed the rifle from him. He was shocked. I pointed the gun at all the men and told them to fix my truck. They jumped to it right away. These men were totally shocked about me; I was unlike any woman of the era. I awoke.

February 5

I was working at WPI factory. For some reason the owner accused me of drinking on the job. I explained to him I haven't had a drink in 40 years and that he was wrong. We argued about it for so long. I was pissed that guy wouldn't listen. I woke.

February 6

I was a rich child – Richie Rich style rich. I and my father – who looked like Richie Rich's dad, lived in a huge house. We lived in excess. I had a fish tank; actually there were fish tanks in every room. I liked my fish tank. One night, my dad took my fish and tank for his own. He replaced mine with an old tank that leaked. The leak was in the upper left-hand corner, the glass was separating. I couldn't get the leak stop. I was mad – downright angry. I went to find my father to yell at him. Every room I went through had plates of candy and cookies. I started grabbing these up. When I found my father he was sitting at a small table that had two chairs. He had a bag of potato chips in his hand and he was wolfing them down. He was crying and couldn't eat them fast enough. I started throwing cookies and candy at him. I was yelling about his excessiveness. I was yelling at him about taking my fish tank. I was pissed! I kept going out of the room and getting more cookies and candy and returning to throw them at him. He never came after me or said a word. I tried to find my way back to my room but couldn't – there were too many rooms. I spotted a dog bed that was full of dog toys. I started throwing them out, there were too many. A household worker saw me and spoke to me about it. I told him there were too many – get rid half of them. Things were too excessive. Then I asked him to show me, guide me, to my room because I couldn't find it. He showed me the way when I got back to my room I awoke.

Note: these dreams leave me grumpy and very tired when I wake up.

February 19

Much detail of this dream was gone by the time I awoke it was a terrible dream!

Everyone I knew and loved was tortured and murdered in front of me. It was one man doing the killing. I don't know how I survived. I believe my husband was one of the first to be killed. If not for this my husband would've done him in. He used many weapons: a gun, knife, rope and baseball bat. I remember crying and screaming. Terrible dream.

February 23

I was a teenager making my first visit to a city. I was alone. I met another teenager and went home with him. He came from a large family. I stayed with his family for a few days. We went out sightseeing and to dance clubs. In his house there where many people and very few bathrooms. In each bathroom beside the toilet was a folding screen and a chamber pot. Whenever I had to go to the bathroom someone was always on the toilet and I had to use a chamber pot.

The last day I was there I had to go pee real bad. I walked into the bathroom and one of the younger boys of the family was on the toilet masturbating. He was wiggling and squirming all over the place. I just said, "hi" and went behind the screen to the chamber pot.. I left the room as soon as possible and apologize for the interruption. A little later the father woke up; he had been sleeping for a week. As he was roaming the house he spotted me and said, "you're still here"? I replied, "I've left and come back since you went to sleep". I woke up I had to pee.

Finally, a dream that wasn't bad.

March 25

It was a hot summer day. I was in the grocery store I think Hannaford's in New London. I saw a blonde woman that looked familiar. I went up to her and said, "Do I know you"? She said, "I think you do. I'm Barbie Boy". I hugged her and said, "I do know you, and I'm Bambi Davis". We chatted a while, then a couple of young boys around 10 and 12 came up the aisle to her. She said, "these are my sons". I was surprised because Barbie boy is my mom's friend, and my mom is 69 years old. After visiting a while, we had a plan to get together for a day. We were going to get mom and dad to join us and go to a beach in Sutton. (I had dreamt of this beach before – beautiful local with many large predatory fish in the water). The next day my husband and I went to where Barbie and her family were staying. (The cabin where she was staying was another place I'd dreamt about before also). In my previous dream, about the cabins, a guy planted some lilies up a trail in the woods. In this dream, the lilies with there. They were orchid looking lilies – they were beautiful. I pointed them out to my husband. I was badly sun burned. I was applying sun block in the parking lot, while waiting for Barbie Boy and her husband. Her kids were outside. They had blobs of sunscreen on them. I helped them spread it on and rub it in. My husband and I walked the path in the woods looking at the lilies, while we were waiting. Barbie boy came out of her cabin started screaming at her kids – it disturbed me terribly. I awoke.

Note: I've had a couple of little dreams since last recorded date. One of which I lost Puppa Chubba and spent the entire dream searching for him. This dream made me anxious.

April 26 – Nap

It was late at night. I was getting ready for bed. The last thing to do was lock the front door. I shut off the outside lights and reached for the lock on the doorknob. All of a sudden the door bust open and a man grabbed my wrist! My heart was ready to burst through my chest! The intruder covered my mouth with his other hand, and dragged me outside. My husband never heard a thing! I struggled with the man. He smelled of alcohol and grease. During the struggle I was able to stomp on the top of his foot. The man let out a howl and hopped around on one foot. I started yelling for my husband. The intruder pushed me, hard. I fell over backwards onto the deck. White lights filled my vision. The man unbuckled his pants and jumped on me. I was in such pain I was helpless. My vision was filled with red and white swirls.

The next thing I knew I was in the hospital. My husband was by my side. I could see policemen waiting on the other side of the curtain. I had dried blood all over me.

I awoke.

June 9

My husband and I were living in a house that was not our present one. I looked out the window one day and saw many exotic animals and wagons coming down the road. I was riveted by them. Walking beside the wagon was one of the most handsome men I'd ever seen. He was beautiful! I went outside to see the animals. The man and his animal stopped at our house. He said, "hi", and I replied back. He asked how I liked his animals and I told him that I love them. He said, "good, I got them just to get your attention". I was shocked at this. He told me his name and said he was from Chile. He then kissed me! I kissed him back! My husband saw this and got really mad. It didn't matter to me; this man from Chile had a spell on me. I left my husband and went with the man. We had many children together and were very happy. One day we went to my old friend, Roberta Fisk's house to visit her. I was surprised to find her home was made into a restaurant. The restaurant was a thriving business. I went upstairs and found her with a group of people visiting. We visited for a while. She said she had to let the restaurant business move in because she couldn't afford the house anymore. She needed to do something. It was great to see Roberta again. I awoke.

Note: In real life, Roberta died many years ago.

June 11

My husband, granddaughter and I were traveling. We stopped at a hotel for the night. I opened the door, at the hotel and there was an adder snake! It was all brown and had a snub tail. While looking at it in shock, and screaming for my husband, it slithered towards me. Then a larger adder came and swallowed the littler one! I freaked out! The snake continued forward into our room. At the doorway it swallowed a mouse. I thought that was good, but was still terrified of the snake. We left the room through a back door and went to a different hotel. (First we told the management about the Adder in the room, and got our money back). The next hotel had a kitchenette in it. Jill stopped by! She opened the back door and showed us a hot tub in the backyard, which went with our room. We were pleased to discover this. Jill left. Then a knock came at the door. I opened the door and it was my daughter. She rushed into my arms crying. She was so upset. When I got her calmed down she told me that the courts had told her that her daughter could not have her last name anymore. I told her this is no big deal; she hasn't raised her daughter anyway. I told her I'd been thinking of changing her name to ours anyway. My daughter was all right with this. She started cooking on the stove. It was some box Chinese meal. She was frying some veggie base and cooking a clear sauce in the saucepan. She stepped away from her cooking. I noticed her messes and that her food was starting to burn. So I took over her cooking and wiped down her messes. When she came back to the stove, to her very well done food, I asked her how she found us. She said she had been following us trying to catch up with us. And that her food was done perfectly. I thought Yuk, on the food. My husband had forgotten something at our other hotel room and tried to call the hotel. He got mad because nobody answered the phone. I reminded him it was too early in the morning for anyone to answer the phone. He agreed. Then I awoke.

June 15

I was living in an apartment in a city. A couple of guys were in the apartment next to me. There was a shared balcony between us. I put a table, chairs and some decorations out on the balcony. It was nice and the guys spent a lot of time out there. We all went to a bar one night. There was a TV there. The guys were watching a movie on the TV. A woman took the remote control, while they weren't looking, and handed it to me. I turned off the TV and hid the remote under me. The guys were mad and looking for the remote. They went to each person in the bar searching for the remote. I showed them my hands to prove I didn't have it, even though I did have it hidden under me. The guys were pissed. I said, "This is a bar. We should have music on and be dancing". Everyone there thought it was a good idea. We danced the night away. The guys owned a restaurant and we went there after being at the bar. Lots of people came into the restaurant to eat. When it was time to close, the guys just left and I was still there. Everything was a mess! The dishes and set ups that were dirty were still on the tables and counter. I cleaned the restaurant then locked up. I thought the guys would like it. When I went home they had moved out which had surprised me. I awoke.

June 16 – Nap

I was driving through Grantham in a four-door yellow boat of a car. My granddaughter was with me, in a car seat in the back. We were searching for a swimming hole that my friend Becky used to swim in. At one of our stops I came across a cat, from our old cat Felony's litter. The cat was a little short haired calico and very happy to see me. The cat came running up to me purring and rubbing on my leg. I put the cat in the car. We started driving down the road and my granddaughter started to cry. I pulled over and got in back with her. I found in the back seat a second steering wheel and a second shifting lever. I started to drive the car from the back seat! Things were going well until I felt I'd get in trouble. I felt that the cops would see nobody in the front seat and two people in the back seat, going down the road. So I pulled over again, to get in the front seat. When I pulled over two girls came over to me. They were close by and thought I had stop to see them. I told them I'd stopped to get in the front seat of the car. They just walked away. When I got out getting in front of the car, the cat got out. She was across the road on an embankment. I went to get her. She was purring.

I awoke because my husband received a phone call.

June 16 – Nap

I set up a yard sale in Grantham. It was strange because it was indoors, and the floor was of sand and a car drove through my stuff. I didn't price anything. Most of my items were glass. When the car came through many of my glass animals were buried in the sand. I got on my hands and knees with two containers: one for those items I wanted to keep and one for those items I wanted to sell. I started grubbing through the sand to find them. There were flowers, houses, a coyote, people, deer, elves, and fish. As I was sorting a woman came in and went right to an old green elephant that was almost a foot long and about 10 inches high. She asked about it. I said that it is old and had been bought by my parents in Germany in 1958. She said she had one already and knew it was valuable. Another woman who owned the building offered to look it up in an antique book to find its value. The elephant wasn't listed. The woman who wanted it offered me $190 and I accepted. The woman started looking over more of my stuff. She found another item she was interested in. The item was a decorative liquor decanter top in the shape of a woman's face with a bonnet on. The woman who bought the elephant offered me $180 for the decanter top – also bought by my parents in 1958 in Germany. She wrote me out a check and put it on the table. I was wrapping up her purchases in a newspaper. The decanter top broke! The woman saw this, I started to cry. She said, "don't worry dear, I want it anyway". She pushed the pieces together and said, "See I can glue it". I thanked her many times over. I decided to pack up and go home. A woman I don't know came by. She helped me load the car.

All of a sudden a man showed up – he looked like John Cusack – I knew he was a soprano type mobster. I grabbed the check off the table and shoved it in my pocket. I told the woman to get in my car. The woman made it to the car. I started for the car and the guy grabbed me. I fought back. I used a wrestling move on him. I had him in a scissor lock. He tried and tried to get free and get me. Each time I applied more pressure. We struggled for a long time. I was trying to figure out how to let go and get to the car safely. Finally I made a decision of what to do. I started piling sand on his face and buried his head in sand. I jumped up and ran for the car. By the time he was up, cleaned up and done coughing I was peeling away in my car. I awoke.

June 22

My husband was a Malcolm in the middle dad type guy. He was making me mad with his foolish behavior. My husband decided our well wasn't good enough. So he hired a well digging guy to come in and rip up the yard. It was such a mess! After a week of digging up the yard, the well digger had gotten no more water than what we had before. My husband figured this was good enough. I said," why did you do this in the first place? Now our yard is totaled". My husband said he'd fix it. His idea was to lay down wood planking to cover up the mess.

Another dream began:

My husband and I were riding in a truck somewhere and he spotted a trailer for sale. He needed a trailer for his work tools so we stopped to look at it. I saw, right away, it was the wrong type of trailer. It looked like a lunch wagon. The sides opened up and there were stainless steel boxes on the sides. There was a backdoor but not enough room inside to get his tools or bike in. When I mentioned that this was the wrong type of trailer he got angry. He said he didn't care, he liked it. I threw my hands up in the air and said, "Whatever" and got back in the truck. I awoke.

June 23

I was back in high school and had my same cubicle. I was full of myself because I had a job in the science department. I was going to get done with that job and go to work for a chiropractor. I saw Debbie H. and got excited, I loved her up. She wanted me to stop; she was trying to surprise someone. Debbie didn't want me to draw attention to her. I was waiting for the bus and remembered my keys were in my cubicle, I needed them. I ran back to my cubicle to get them afraid I'd miss the bus. I was living in the house in Sutton that was the Rowe's. This house was right across the street from where my grandparents used to live. Someone had bought my grandparents house. The place looked terrible; it looked like it was going to fall in! The new people were painting the house green. I was pissed. I wanted the house destroyed. I went over and argued with the new owners and told them to destroy the house. They wanted to know why. I told them about getting sexually assaulted there. They told me, "too bad" and continued to paint. I was selling the Rowe house. I had a tea set to sell in order to have fewer things to move. A man came to look at the house and tea set. One teacup was not part of the set, the cup was very large. The man said, "How much for the cup? I want to break it". I said, "$100". He said, "That's nothing. I buy my clothes on installments. I paid $321 per installment". I thought, "Wow", and awoke.

June 24 – Nap

My husband and I lived at Battle's farm. The woman who used to own it was still there. She had five horses: three Brown, one gray and a beautiful black that had white spots on its chest. She would take them, each day, to pasture somewhere. Each night she would bring them home. They were like big dogs, very obedient. My husband talked with some guy about motorcycles. The woman at the farm told me about gold in the hillside. A mouse had brought a piece down. I awoke.

Nap

Puppa, my dog, and I were at some school where my mother was working in the kitchen. There was a trough for the dishes. Puppa got in the trough and peed! He also peed on the leg of the school lunch table. I was mortified! I ran into the kitchen grabbing some paper towels and stuffed them into my pockets. I then went to the trough and used the hose to wash away the Pee. Mom saw me using the hose and said, "Isn't that great! I love it". I agreed that it was very nice. I went to the cafeteria sopped up Puppa's pee before anyone noticed it. I awoke.

June 25 – Nap

Wayne M. brought me a gift. The gift was a funny little walking duck. Wayne was not alone. He had a classmate of mine with him. I couldn't think of her name in my dream and I can't remember her name now. I was wearing a bathing suit with a hospital Johnny over it. He took us to a house that was on the lake. When I got out of the car I thought I had forgotten Puppa. Then Puppa jumped out of the car. I was relieved. Then I discovered I had forgotten my cigarettes. As we were going inside I asked, "Where is Sue"? Wayne said, "Oh she likes to shop – shop for alcohol". I said, "oh"! Puppa came in the house and peed. I was a gasp! I grabbed him up and took him outside. He started running with some other dogs. They jumped in the lake. The lake was deep. I saw a beautiful goldfish. I was afraid that Puppa couldn't swim across the cove. I was ready to jump in but he made it with the other dogs. I awoke I had to pee.

June 25 - Dream #2

My husband and I were in bed at night. He wouldn't stop kicking the mattress. Being in a waterbed the vibration went throughout the whole bed. I kept asking him to stop but he wouldn't. I was getting very mad. Finally, (and really), I got out of bed and grab the top blanket off the bed. I was going to sleep on the floor. (This was at 5:12 AM. My husband woke and said, "What the hell! you been dreaming, dammit. I might as well get up now, I'm awake thanks"!

Dream #3

Kenny G. and I were in my car. We went out to the town clerk's office. The exterior of the town clerk's office had changed. There was a balcony where a door used to be. We stepped out of the car to examine the entrance. We were just a few feet away from my car and someone stole it! We went to the police station to file a report, and it was Jim V. I had to deal with. Afterwards we started walking home. At some point Kenny turned into Jeff H. We went through a yard and the people wanted to eat my dog, Puppa Chubba. I fought for his life! It was terrible! The whole family wanted to eat my dog! There were lots of them. I kicked and fought through every room of their house. I put Puppa in my pocket so I could fight better. I beat them with anything I could find. I smashed heads, broke bones and fought like my life depended on it! I don't know what happened to Kenny/Jeff I left him behind. I finally made it out of there. I got on a train, thinking oh I'm safe. I took Puppa out of my pocket, concerned he might be dead. He was still alive but, barely. On the train we had to stand in compartments. I was leery of which one to be in. I was afraid someone would still be out to get us. So I chose a compartment that had an old lady in it. When the doors closed she turned to me and smiled. She had cannibal pointed teeth. I reached for the window and she bit my hand. I pulled my hand back and saw slashes across my fingers. Then a face appeared in the window of a guy with cannibal teeth. He said, "oh, cancer, fresh cancer". At that point I gave up. I awoke.

June 26

I showed someone how to kill and dress 2 turkeys.

Dream #2

My husband and I were with a couple that was getting married.

Dream #3

I was with Mike, Jodi, and Suzy in a boathouse. Mike dove in the water. I said, "the water is not deep". Suzy jumped in the water and it wasn't up to her knees. Puppa was there, I had to lift him onto the dock in the boathouse by his collar. I awoke.

June 27 – Nap

Mom and dad gave my granddaughter a 35mm camera. My granddaughter had opened the back of it. I looked and saw the film was all done. We ran it around, taped it up and put it in the bag, ready for developing.

Note: my husband came home and woke me up.

June 27 – Evening

I spent the night fighting off drag queens. They were putting on a musical and kept stealing my frillies. I had so many frilly nighties – all colors styles and patterns. Those drag queens wanted them all. One would dart in and grab a handful. I'd go after him and others would go after my clothes while my attention was on the other. Finally, I gave up and let the drag queens have my clothes. They all tried to wear my stuff and found that none of it fit. Conflict over.

Note: I've been in the hospital and had dreams but by the time I got home the memory is gone.

July 4

I had lost my bottom denture and needed a new one made. I had to weave my way through many rooms. There were so many rooms I needed a guide to get me where I was going. When I got to where the person was with my lower denture, I was upset. They had used a green plastic instead of flesh colored for the gum. There were lots of knots all over it because the teeth were tied in. I didn't want green gums but it fit well. I awoke.

July 6

I was walking down a road to go visit my friend Cheryl. It was a nice country road. There were other people with me. We walked past a lot that had three geometric domes on it. All three domes were made of an aluminum foil type material. I could see small openings around each triangle. I said, "if they'd fill those cracks the domes would be more efficient". One dome was one person's bedroom and medium-sized. One dome was a couple's bedroom and it was the largest. The last dome was the smallest and was a bathroom. We got to Cheryl's place, a farm. It'd been raining and a stream ran by the barn, the stream was ankle-deep. The next thing I knew the stream was 5 feet deep. A baby fell into the stream and no one was going in after it! I jumped in to rescue the baby.

The dream changed:

I was in the hospital! I was going to have surgery! I was playing with the controls on the bed, trying to get it a certain way. A nurse came in to check me before surgery. She marked my face with a pen. I asked, "why?" and she replied, "to see if you lose weight". I told her, "I have a cold in my chest and can't have anesthesia". The nurse replied, "Don't worry, it'll be all right". I woke.

July 8

I went back to WPI factory to get a job. They remembered me and hired me for a night job. My husband, granddaughter and I went to visit Dave S. and Mike A. They were living in a house that was falling apart. To get to this place, you had to drive through a fallen down place. There were boards with nails on the ground. My granddaughter and I went to clear away these boards. My granddaughter was lying down while moving boards. My husband came driving through – I threw something at his passenger-side window to make him veer away. I thought he was going to run over our granddaughter! While we were there visiting the guys, one of their grandmothers came to visit. She was naked and proud of it! My God! Dave S. said, "This is why we live out here", pointing to the naked woman. We got in the truck and took a ride up a logging road. We went around a corner; in front of us was a cliff of ash, covered with birds. The birds were eagles. There were so many of them living in the cliff of ash. Looking around, the cliff was like a bowl and there were hundreds of eagles living there. I awoke.

July 9

I was in school – I think middle school. It was time to go home. The other kids and I got on the bus. A couple kids were supposed to come home with me. Their parents were not going to be home. Only one kid got off the bus with me. There was supposed to be two kids coming home with me. The other kid and I went to my house. It was boring, the adults were watching hunting shows on TV and we were not interested. We went out to play. A second bus came by; I got on it to speak with the boy who didn't get off with us. I asked him, "What's up? Why didn't you get off the bus with us"? He said, "I want to just stay on the bus". He lay down on the bus seat and started reading a book. I said to him, "You know you have zero social abilities. I know this, because I am like that too." I awoke.

July 10

I was working somewhere, which was like a printing place. I had a workstation. I had to proof read some stuff. I had equipment that was very magnetic to work with. One day I came into work and my equipment was covered in iron filings. There were so many iron filings my work station was unusable. It was terrible! Someone had sabotaged my workstation! I was crying. This became a mystery. I tried to discover who the person was that did this to me. At one point I got on the ground and looked across the floor. There were military rings, (jewelry), in the grooves of the floor. I figured it was a military person who did this to my work station. I lifted my work mat and there was an odd curved knife under the mat. A tall Indian man, who was a maintenance man, came by to help clean my work station. He kissed me! I told him that my husband isn't going to like this. He stopped. My coworkers were sympathetic about my station being wrecked by iron filings. I awoke.

July 16 – Dream #1

I was applying for a job with Oprah Winfrey. There were many people in the waiting area, applying for the same job. As soon as a person would go in for their interview, they would come right back out. It was my turn; I was wearing my light green dress. I went in and said, "Hi", to Oprah. She said, "hi, what a nice dress. I think you should be sitting on something beige, to go with your dress. Go out to the waiting room and find something beige, bring it back in and we will continue our interview". I was thrilled to have a chance. I went out into the waiting room and started rummaging around looking for something that was beige colored. I found a stack of fabric and some was beige. I took the material back in to continue my interview. The dream ended.

Dream #2

I was young person again, living with my brothers at mom and dad's. The IRS was going to take the house in a few days. We were rummaging through the house to find the most important things to take with us. We took personal files, money, jewelry, and some clothes, anything that we really needed. I awoke.

July 18

My husband and I had an apartment. We were going to move out and were packing up the place. We had half the apartment packed. We decided to take a walk. We walked down the road; we saw every home had a cow or ox. I saw one team of oxen that had a golden harness. I was very impressed by their good health and harness get up. I did wonder why they were harnessed up and standing in their stall. We walked on and ended up at home. When we got home we decided to keep our apartment until May. I went out to tend to our cow that lived in the garage. The landlord came by. I asked the landlord if we could stay until May. She saw the cow in the garage and said certainly, seeing how you have a cow. I asked her what was up with every home having a cow. The landlord replied, "Peregrine falcons need the cow manure, crap, to live. The state requires us to have them to help increase the population. The Fish and Game department says they are endangered". I awoke.

July 19

I was walking down the road toward a neighbor's house. A cop stops and frisks me! In my left hand pants pocket is a bag of pot seeds. The cop wants to bust me. I looked at him like he was an idiot and said, "What? These are bird seeds". This made the cop stop and think. He said, "why do you have them with you"? I asked him to follow me and he did. I went to the neighbors and there were at least half-dozen birdfeeders. I took the seeds and put them in the feeders and said, "see". He didn't like this. From then on cops were watching me everywhere. I couldn't go anywhere without them spying on me.

Then things changed over to another dream.

For some reason a bunch of people put on a play for me. I now have forgotten the title. There was a dinner served as well. I didn't like anything they served. I had a child with me, maybe seven or eight years old, somewhere around there. During the play I was so bored and wanted to leave. So the kid and I snuck out. I awoke.

July 20 – A.M. Nap

My husband was building us a new house.(I don't know what the outside looks like). I was giving someone a tour of the inside. The house was at the newly sheet rocked stage. In the corner was a window screen and adjacent was an outlet. The outlet was weird because it had a little fish tank below it. The little tank only had a few fish in it. I was looking at the fish when I notice there were black spiders behind the screen. There were only two and I kicked them to kill them. More spiders came out from somewhere. I kicked those. The first ones, I thought I killed, started to move! I kicked them again. More spiders came out! All the ones I thought I killed were moving! I went and got an insecticide spray to kill them. I put my

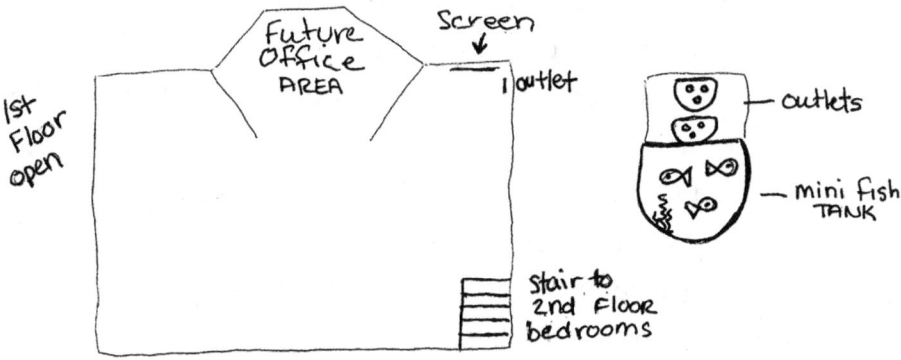

hand over the fish tank as I sprayed – hoping I wasn't going to kill the fish. I awoke.

Dream #2

Jill and I were at a high school talent show. Max was doing a play. I was sick and in my bathrobe. I was worried about my bathrobe. Then a man passed by wearing, what looked like, a bathrobe too. It was really a fur coat. When the show began I sat in a chair beside Jill. First up was a dance team, interpretive dance, I guess. They sucked. Next was a student's video production. It was great! Jill and I commented on it to each other. Next we knew, a man was jumping over the chairs, from behind us. He was excited about our comments and wanted to talk to us about it. Max's play was the best of everything. I went home to my one room. It was dirty – I was ill but had to start picking the place up. People came in and started taking my things! I had to argue and fight with everyone to leave my stuff alone! I awoke.

July 24

I was in a hospital (really I was). There were six other women who stayed with me. One night we stayed outdoors. I saw Shaggy and had a short visit with him. I didn't find out if he had his baby yet. My granddaughter was with me, everyone loved her. People kept taking turns feeding her. One day a challenged girl, from the hospital, wanted to feed her. I allowed it with supervision. While that child was feeding my granddaughter I went outside for a walk. I spotted Jeff H. dragging a wooden wheelchair. In the chair was my daughter with only a shirt on! I ran to her to give her a hug she said, "no mom stop"! I did. She was taking a bloody shit and had crap all over herself. She had a clear bowl in her mouth that had blood bubbling in it. "The blood! " She said. We went indoors to a private meeting area. My daughter wanted to see her daughter. In the meantime Obama came in. He came over to me and hugged me. I was grossed out! He had a booger flapping and was wearing one of those goatees with a hair tie in it, like Lou Albano used to. Then he called Jeff's name. Jeff came over and picked him up taking him to his chair, on the other side of the room. I went to that side of the room and asked Obama what his problem was. Obama said, "my feet". He took his feet out of his fancy loafers and his white silk socks. The soles of his feet were covered in blood! I gasped and said, "let me get you some ice". As I was approaching the ice machine, to get the gross/bloody Obama ice, there was my daughter. She had brought her daughter a pair of culottes (shorts/skirt cross). On the back of the culottes said Emily or Emily Rose. I looked at them and said, "what's up with this"? Then someone came in and woke me up.

July 25 – in the Hospital

My husband and I were at a rest stop on the highway somewhere. There were many trained animals there, mostly horses, for a show of some kind. We found a place to park, to get out and stretch our legs; we were near a beautiful draft horse. The horse was huge with black mane and tail and chestnut hide. We approached him; we came at him straight on. We did not want to surprise him. All of a sudden his front hoof came forward, like pointing. I don't know if it struck my husband or if he jumped back from it. When my husband went backwards he crashed into two big guido looking guys from New

York, or someplace. Those guidos pulled their knives! I get scared because I knew where this competition was going. My husband smiled and got in his truck. He drove across the parking lot to be right across from us. He got out of the truck and displayed a four sided target. I tapped the guys, who thought their little display had scared my husband away. I told them to look across the way. As my husband turned the target from side to side it seemed to spell out a message, to the guidos. I could see their eyebrows going up. My husband then reached down and retrieved a very impressive pistol; he pointed it at the guidos. I smiled and said to them, "My husband's a competition shooter, he wins all the time. Are you sure you want to bring knives to a gunfight"? The guidos looked at my husband and put their knives away. I said, "Good decision boys". My husband just smiled, nodded and got back in his truck. The guidos and I sat against the concrete wall to talk. I explained to them what the horse had done and that my husband didn't intentionally bump into them. They understood and apologized. I could see that these were just a couple of fat, insecure city boys, it was kind of comical. As I'm sitting there I notice money on the ground, coins. There are people standing on top of the money so I just waited for the people to leave. When they did walk away I bent down and gathered the money. There were half dollars and quarters mostly. I was surprised at how much money there was. The guidos started looking around and found home accent pieces. They got out boxes and started packing the home accent pieces away. One piece had Native Americans all around it, one had a chicken – these were in silhouette and painted black. The fat boys from the city were so happy. They loaded the car with boxes of stuff and drove off smiling and waving. I went, happily, to my husband's truck with fists full of money I had found.

My husband was happy; he'd made an impression on those fat boys. I awoke due to the nurses coming into my room.

July 26 – still in the Hospital

My car broke down by a Russian Embassy. I walked to it to see about getting some help. The building was like a John S. /Fred Flintstone concrete bunker, interesting style. I knocked at the door and there was no answer, so I pushed on the door and found it open. I went inside and hollered hello. There was no answer so I started looking around for a phone. The place was nice and neat but simple. I went into a room and discovered an indoor pool. It looked great. There was a lot to it, not just your average rectangle. The pool went everywhere and had lots of things in it. Things like hammocks, seats and toys. I couldn't resist, I stripped-down to my least amount of clothes and jumped in. The water was wonderfully warm and clear. I was able to keep my eyes open without them burning. I checked everything out. The chairs and the hammocks seem sexual to me. I moved on to see what else was around. I came to a section, around a bend that was like an arcade. I tried one of the games – it was a driving game. I had to pump the pedals with my feet – like a pump organ only standing, kind of like an underwater jogger. A monitor came on that had a car moving around the track. There was another driving game beside that one. A man showed up and started playing on that one. I was a little concerned because I just made myself to home, uninvited. We waved to each other. There were other underwater games there, so I moved along. I played some other game, I don't remember what it was because a beautiful blonde woman came up and played beside me and I was distracted. Things seem to become a competition between the man and the woman, to see who could get my attention the most. The woman was so voluptuous and beautiful, the man went away hangdog. I didn't make any clear decisive moves toward either of them; I just continued to check out the pool. I moved along into another underwater room. This one seems to be set up like a sports arena. There were game areas, but each area had bleachers. There was an underwater concession stand (weird). Because I was kind of ignoring the blonde woman, and had had more interest in the pool and equipment, she started to hang her head and hang back from my exploring. I felt bad. I found a balance horse that had handles like a gymnastic horse. I grab the handles and just stiffened my body and did presses up and down. It was pretty easy because it was underwater. The blonde saw me doing this and came to join me, (blush). She started doing the same presses as I was in sync with me. People started gathering and sitting on the bleachers. Those people were cheering and clapping. The blonde and I were bumping breasts when we were reaching the up position.

My dream changed:

I was in a shed/barn looking for a cat. I saw one that was solid gray. I wanted it, so I grabbed it up. It really wasn't gray. It was covered in gray shit. I awoke

August 1

My son and I were driving through Newport one summer evening. All of a sudden my son yelled at me, 'mom pullover". I did and right beside us was an Asian fellow. My son said, "Are you Jet Li"? The man replied, "Yes, please hide me from the people". We let him in the back seat. He slumped down so fans wouldn't see him. I thought this was all strange because nobody was swarming him – I didn't even know who he was. The weirdest thing about him was the winter coat he was wearing. It was so hot out and yet he was cold. I figured that there must be a major climate difference between here and wherever he was from. My son was thrilled to be with Jet Li. Mr. Li said he was hungry. So I drove to a Chinese restaurant. We were led into a private room when I explained, to the owners, that Jet Li wanted to not be bothered. In front of the door, to the private room, a sleeping bag looking thing hung to hide the door. A few people were in the room when we went in. A few of the owner's friends and family wanted to meet Jet Li. When we were seated, I asked Jet Li why he was wearing a heavy winter coat in our summer. I awoke.

END OF VOLUME 2

VOLUME 3

August 6

I was at an outdoor bar sitting at a table. I was waiting for my husband and granddaughter to arrive. I was also waiting for the band to start. The waitress brought me a bottle of soda, I think a Sprite. A couple arrived; I think it was one of the waitresses from the Bradford Junction and her husband. They were all bummed out. I asked what the problem was and she replied, "Oh we've been sick. We've had colds and he hurt his foot. Things are really terrible". I said, "Don't let it get you down. I've been in the hospital twice this month for grand mal seizures". Next they were complaining about their grown children. I laughed. This made them mad. I said, "at least they didn't have a baby and drop it off for you to raise". They looked at each other and said, "my God"! I just smiled and drank my soda. There was a little piece of paper under the cap of my soda. I had a couple of other papers with me, to get them checked. There was a contest with the soda company. So I had the waitress check the papers I had. Two of them were only worth points you redeem online. The third was a picture of a green guy like the Hulk and was worth $250 worth of merchandise. The waitress started to bring pizzas, drinks and what all. I took a walk down a grassy road right near the bar. I thought this would be a good place for my granddaughter to hang out, not too loud, not too many people, perfect. When I looked back at the spot where I was sitting there was $250 worth of stuff sitting there. I wasn't going to check it out until my husband showed up with my granddaughter. I woke.

August 7 – Nap

Mom, dad, my husband, granddaughter, Puppa and I moved into a big house together. The house was huge, and fancy. My husband and I selected our bedroom. Next-door to our bedroom room was a room that I selected for an office. Mom decided that the room would make a good office for her too. I had no problem with that at all. One day I got a lot of mail for one of my clients, he was behind on all his payments to the state and the IRS. I walked into the office with all the mail and mom was there writing on a white line paper. I apologize for bothering her she replied, "No problem, I'm done. Where's the baby"? I said, "She is with the sitter, a few rooms away". "Ah good, I wanted to read this to you". We both sat down on the floor, side-by-side. Basically what the paper said was mom was dying. There was some other stuff on the paper but my brain shut down after the dying part. We grabbed each other and started crying. We cried and cried in each other's arms. Finally we were cried out. I asked mom if I could take that white paper and reread it again when I could wrap my brain around it better. She agreed and left the room. The phone rang and it was mom. I was surprised and confused because she had just left the room. She laughed and said, "Come out of the room". As I got to the door way there was mom. She said, "Look at this" pushing a curtain back. There was a security control pad, a telephone and a key rack. The phone could call outside like a regular phone or call internally. On the key rack were some pennies. They had copper wire wrapped around their outer edge and then hung by a loop. I thought what the hell, these seem worthless. I checked to see if there were any wheaties, there weren't. I just left them alone. Next someone playing the guitar beautifully distracted me from the things hidden in the corner by the curtain. I started looking around to see who was playing the guitar. What a shock! It was dad! I had no idea he could play. He never played while we kids were growing up. I had no idea! I asked him why the big secret. He said the schedule he had to keep playing in the clubs was too much once he and mom had started a family. Mom smiled ear to ear. He said the drugs were getting too much for him too. At this point he stopped playing and opens the closet door. He got on the closet rod and hung upside down by his knees. The blood started rushing to his head. He began reciting all the drugs he used to do: blues, reds, poppers... I awoke.

Note: In reality, my father did not do any drugs unless they were prescribed to him.

August 8

Some girlfriends and I bought a café in a big city. We did inventory, many things were junk and had to be thrown out. In the walk-in there was a side and whole beef that was good. That made me real happy. The equipment was good, but the place was run down. We knew that with a little spit shine the cafe' could be up and running soon. After spending the day hauling things out and cleaning, I decided to go for walk with Puppa. We set out, not knowing where we were going, just exploring. I didn't walk, I skated along, without any means; like on wheels or blades. Puppa had to work to keep up with me. I went down one street and found it to be a dead end. There was a very handsome black man there. He had the most beautiful smile. When he saw me he said, "Sorry this is a dead-end". I replied,

"I don't mind, it was worth coming down to see a handsome man like you". I didn't think anything of saying this because I'm 50 and he was a young man. I didn't think he'd take my compliments seriously. He just waved, blushed, and smiled. I turned around and skated off with Papa running behind me. We continue to explore the city skating away. After a little while the handsome black man came skating up to me. We skated some of the streets together. Then I asked him if he had wheels on. He replied that he did and showed them to me. I said cool. I don't have anything on my shoes, I can just glide. I was surprised that he made an effort to seek me out. He took my hand, I blushed, and we continued on. After a while I got tired and wanted to go back to my café. I didn't know where I was, I was lost! I had to ask directions to get back to the cafe'. The young black man and Puppa went back to the café with me. I awoke.

August 10

I got a job in Vermont, I was so happy. I was working in the test department of the toy company. I got the job the same day I applied. They were training me. The test department was like a sunken living room. It had shag carpet and worked two shifts. We were testing monkeys. There was a battery, (like a car battery), with clips to hook to each and every monkey, before shipping. After checking the motion of the monkeys we would move them over to the next battery and check the audio. I noticed the motion was going during the audio check also. So I asked, "Why do two checks? Why not do one test for both functions"? "Oh good idea that'll save us lots of time, we're glad we hired you", said the management. The next shift came in. I noticed the steps up to the main floor were covered in pile. I was able to scoop up in my arms a whole armful of pile to throw in the trash. I asked, "When was the last time this place was cleaned up"? Nobody knew. The factory was so cool. We could smoke and there was an open bar, very surprising. When it was time to go I couldn't find my car. There were many parking lots. One of my coworkers asked me where I came from. I replied, "Newbury New Hampshire". My coworker said he commuted from Boston each day. I thought: oh my God, this must be a great job. I continued to search for my car. I awoke

Note: very odd that I keep dreaming about bars, I quit drinking in 1979.

August 12

Cheryl and I were taking care of a bunch kids. This wasn't just babysitting. These kids would be fostered by us or orphans. My granddaughter was with them. We all slept on the floor in one room. Some of the little ones fell asleep with no blankets and lay there shivering. I got the kids some blankets and pillows. One big girl came over and fell asleep near me. She snored with her mouth open. I could see all of the cavities in her teeth. I could also see how dirty she was, she needed a bath badly. When we got up, Cheryl and I took the children to a lake for a swim. Things were going great until a lifeguard there said he stepped on something crunchy and wondered what it was. I stuck my head underwater and took a look around – I saw catfish,(small ones), and angelfish looking fish, maybe silver dollar fish. I couldn't see anything else, but I kept looking. All of a sudden I saw an eel! I jumped out of the water and told the lifeguard that I saw an eel! I told him, "This Lake had an eel problem before. The state had salted the lake to get rid of eels. These eels were weird: they had a big mouth and legs, they had evolved! I started getting the kids out of the water. The eels were chasing us! Puppa was bitten, but got away without too much damage. The eels were putting a painkiller into its victims, so there would be no pain when bitten. The eels were walking right out of the water, chasing us. When the eels came out of the water, we stomped on them. Some of the kids didn't get out of the water right away. They got bitten by the eels. The bites seem to paralyze them. Those bitten were sinking in the water. We were frantically trying to rescue the children. I got bit hauling the last two kids out. Those two kids were underwater a little while and paralyzed. I got them to shore and was stomping eels at the same time. The eels were awful. The paralyzed children came around but nobody was happy. I awoke.

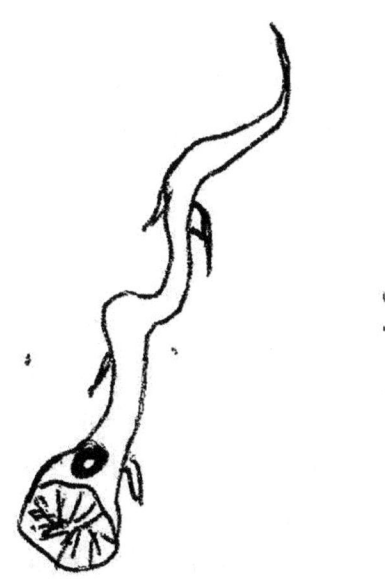

August 15

I was listening to a radio auction show. It was around Christmas time and my children still lived at home. A TV came up for auction. The auctioneer said it was 11" x 17" and I thought he said 11" x 70". So I bid $167.50, which was ridiculous! Well of course I won the TV. When a couple of guys came to deliver the TV, my mother- in- law was visiting. The men brought extra stuff with them. They called me their platinum purchaser. They were hanging Christmas ornaments around the house. This is when I realized I had greatly overpaid. The guys who delivered the TV started rearranging the house. The kids were getting upset. The kids were trying to put things back the way they were, things were chaos. My mother-in-law wanted to do some laundry. She held her clothes in the shower and turned it on. The water was spraying everywhere, what a mess! I yelled for my husband to fix it, but for some reason, he couldn't. I had to get all wet and try to reposition the spray. Water was everywhere! The bathroom was soaked. A couple of inches of water was everywhere, floors, walls, ceiling, and on fixtures. I was mad. My mother-in-law acted like nothing had happened. She gathered her clothes, whistling away and left. I was steaming mad. My husband woke me up.

August 21

My husband, my two children and I were riding around looking for something to do. We came across a hot tub water park. We thought that would be just right, as long as the tubs weren't too hot. I didn't have a swimsuit with me. All I had with me were 2 white tank tops! I thought, if I wore one on top of the other I'd be all right. We went into the tubs and they were just right. There were many tubs in a row, in different shapes and a maze. The tubs had radios and waitresses. My husband started drinking all kinds of drinks. They kept track of the tabs by printing out a brochure, looking thing, which listed all the ingredients. The kids were having fun due to the music and other kids there. I was having trouble with my white tank tops. When I went into the first tub, my tank tops floated up, so I was exposed! As my husband's list of drinks got longer and more varied, we decided to go up to another level of tubs. To get there we had to ride an escalator. We climbed on; there was a bunch of teenagers in front of us. One of the teenage boys was arguing with a girl. When they reached the top, the boy pushed the girl back down. She fell a story or two and landed on her back. We called 911. She was really hurt. I awoke.

August 23

I had a dream but the phone ringing in the morning made me lose it. :-(

August 24

I was in the town that Johnny Depp was in. He was out and about. He had a book signing and nobody showed up! He went to some other social event and people were talking behind his back. I was thrilled to see him, but most were treating him like a has been. I went over and spoke to him! I don't recall our conversation but I do recall his ego getting larger and larger. As the evening passed, it got disgusting. I left him with his own best friend, himself.

The dream seemed to skip into another.

I was taking lots of photos of my granddaughter. She was a toddler. I had a video recorder and was trying to take just clips with her in it. A woman was putting on a play and my granddaughter was in it. She was dressed in a little Native American costume. The woman was upset with me, for only wanting to take video with my granddaughter in it. The bottom part of the camera was slow to view the play. The top part of the camera was faster, showing thumbnails. The woman showed me these features on the camera and then huffed off, when she saw what I was doing. She felt I should have been interested in her whole play. A doorway was the stage. I awoke.

August 25

My husband and I had a big house. One of those houses so big you need a full-time person to help you run it. So big you had a commercial kitchen in it. Our wait staff – help – was Antonio Bandera. My husband and I were outside, I went inside for something. There was Antonio. He easily seduced me into bed. I didn't want to, but he was so alluring. Afterwards, I fell asleep. My husband came in and wanted to know what I was doing. I told him I had fallen asleep. Antonio came into the room, to do something. I had started to feel guilty about the affair, but Antonio touched his necklace. Then I noticed the necklace was strangely shaped and not metal. He had used his necklace on me! I sighed with relief, that we had not really had sex –not with him physically, just an object. My husband laid down with me and we both went to sleep. After we got up and went into the kitchen to look it over, it was beautiful. Things were mostly stainless steel and I saw a huge Hobart mixer. I awoke.

August 26

My husband and I went to Springfield to look at a house, to rent. It was right on the backside of Lake Kollimook. I was very happy about that. The house was oddly arranged. The house was also furnished. In the living room was a collection of stuffed owls – many kinds. The bathroom was sunken, which was so odd. We were thinking of renting it. While we were looking at it, for the first time, a guy came in who had rented it before. But we got there first. The owner said the house needed work. A foot had to be removed from the bathroom; it was on the neighbor's property. That was going to be a big job. We went back inside, to look again. The owls were alive. The blankets on the beds were floating. The house was haunted.

I went into another dream

My husband had gotten his deer, a nice 12 point buck. He had it in the back of his truck. It was big and he had the back open so people could see it. We drove around through Market Basket grocery store with it, so people could see it. I awoke.

August 28

My husband and I went to Mexico. We saw a couple of kids there, a boy and a girl. They were around eight or nine years old. We saw them at a store. The store had very little to buy in it. The kids were just hanging in the street. We tried to get them out of the street. We thought they'd get struck by a car. They wanted to come with us. They were filthy. We put them in our truck and asked them where they lived. They pointed to their house. We went there and saw their parents. The parents told us we could have the kids. An older teenage girl came out and said she wanted to come with us too. We took them all. I thought the older one could help care for our granddaughter. We started to leave and then I remembered we know nothing about the kids – name – dates of birth – Social Security numbers. So we went back to the parent's house. The parents invited us in. I got a pen and paper out and sat at the table to get the information. The parents said to call the kids what we wanted, the little girl was Jean and they had no Social Security numbers and little to no schooling. The parents were trying to remember the dates of birth when I noticed the house was crawling. There were bugs and maggots everywhere! They were on the floor, on the table – everywhere! My husband woke me up.

August 29

I'm in the hospital,(in my dream). It's New London, the beds were terrible. At one point I was sitting in a chair they took my bed away! I had pneumonia. I ended up having to go into the hospital three times. Back to back to back, all for the same thing. The last time I was in there they were going to transport me to Henniker. I had two different blood pressures in my lungs. One lung had one and the other had another! I was about to get transferred, I was outside waiting for a ride. I was having a cigarette when my husband came.

He had a small wound. He was going to go into the hospital and have them tend to it. I said don't bother, I could do it. On the outside wall of the hospital was a clear plastic box that contained medical supplies. In one bin were Band-Aids. I had to scrounge around to find the cloth type that my husband likes. I took two of those,(they were darker brown than the plastic type). On the shelf next to the band-aids were other supplies. I looked them over and saw antiseptic wipes, Novocain, needles, Betadine. I grabbed the Betadine. I awoke.

August 30

I went to visit my father in Springfield. I could see back by the turkey coop was a mess. There was a trailer, a pile of logs, a couple of dogs. A guy was supposed to be logging. While I was visiting, a guy showed up with a couple of long pieces of rebar. It was so long he drag them around the front lawn, they were like a plow. The rebar dug up the whole front lawn! I was pissed! I went outside screaming. I told that guy to get his shit and leave right now! "Whatever you're doing is done ! Get your stuff and get out"! Dad came out of the house and asked what was going on. I said," look at the lawn". He nodded his head at the guy, who agreed it was time to pick up and go. What a mess, I was ranting and raving! I went out back to look at what was going on. Dad came with me. He sat down at a card table that had two chairs. He was talking to someone across the table, may be my husband. I noticed that I had a pipe in my mouth the whole time. I'd bitten on the stem! I noticed a dog was barking up a storm, a black and tan. I asked how many dogs were here. Dad replied, "24!" I asked, "why so many dogs"? Dad said, "These are special dogs, they are porpoise detectors". I said, "what – there are no porpoises around here". The other dogs were behind the trailer. The man was loading up his gear and started to haul it away. I was looking around, there was so much garbage. The trash angered me so much. While I was looking around I looked at Dad's profile and noticed his teeth. It took me awhile to figure out what was different. He had had a bottom plate put in, the denture was odd. The angle of the bottom teeth were like horse bottom teeth – angled out. It made Dad's speech and face different. My husband was asking what the guy was doing back there by the turkey coop. Dad said logging. My husband asked, "why the trailer and dogs? Why the rebar"? Dad couldn't answer. The guy was up to something more than logging. What a mess, they laughed. Boy, I was pissed. I awoke.

August 30 - Afternoon Nap

I went outside the house to have a smoke and pay some bills. There was a desk and chair outside. I had my checkbook and cigarettes in hand. I sat down and looked around. I noticed another checkbook that looks very much like mine. I went and picked it up and looked inside. The checks were gone but the extra deposit slips left when you are done were there. I thought it was Joe S.'s, even though that was not the name I read (odd). I went and hollered inside the house, "Joe, I found your checkbook". Joe was visiting my husband. I returned to the table and chair. There was a glass of red wine on the table, the glass was half full. I sat down to write a check. A young woman, who was quite cute and perky, arrived on her bicycle. I didn't speak; she just smiled at me and went to the door. My husband let the woman in. I was wondering about the woman and my husband when Aunt Lily showed up. It was good to see her. She mentioned that Marlene and I used to play when we were children. She asked me how old I was now. She thought I was 48; I corrected her, telling her I was 51. She said that Uncle Harry had thought, now that I was older, I could have a few of the family things. I don't know what she meant by that statement. She left and got into her car.

The dog yelped and I awoke.

August 31

I was at a farm that had three horses. One was a bay, one was a beautiful gray and one was just nondescript brown. People were riding the horses, all at a walk. I thought good, that gray will be all warmed up when it was my turn. When it became my turn, for some reason the horses were turned out. I had to go into the barn and locate the bridle and saddle; the former riders were riding bareback. I wanted a nice canter around, so I wanted a saddle, for the use of the stirrups. I went into the barn and things were strange. I had to pass through a pickup truck to get to the horses area. The truck was brand-new and was green. The interior was ripped out of it. When I got in the truck it felt like it was moving. It was an odd feeling; I had to make sure it wasn't moving. I got to the horse area and the ground was underwater. The horses had no problem with this, but I did, it was deep. I had to stand on a thin ledge of ground. There were two bridles; I didn't know which one was for the gray. One bridle had tape all over it. I asked the owner and she didn't reply. The farm help was asleep, in bed's, in another part of the barn. I couldn't find a saddle at all. Oh well. I started to try the bridle without tape on the gray. That bridle had sunglasses on it for the horse, I thought that's nice. I awoke.

September 1

Note: this seems to me, to be a reoccurring dream – but I have not written about it before. I don't know when I would've dreamt this before. When I had the dream, last night, that was the feeling that came with it, I can't fully describe the dream.

It involves my granddaughter and racism. I argued with someone about her unknown heritage. That someone seemed KKK-ish, but I don't know. This dream is very vague. I awoke.

September 3 – midnight

Note: I didn't think I was asleep. I only went to sleep at 10:00 PM. I was tossing and turning. I lay with both my hands clasped on my chest. Next to me, on the right, my dog laid snuggled up to me. Further on my right, lay my husband. We have a king size bed. I could hear my husband and dog breathing. Then I heard another person breathing on my left. I felt someone was standing beside me! I felt them duck down beside me. I felt someone hold my hand. (My hands were clasp on top of each other and this other person's hand was on top of mine)! The person was ducked down so that if my husband reached over to try and feel the other person, he wouldn't be able to. I spoke my husband's name, "someone is holding my hand"! I said it again, I was frightened. I truly said these words aloud.

My husband woke and shown his flashlight over me. I was glad to see no one was really there. I feel I was not asleep. I got up and came downstairs to write this, still feeling I was awake. This was scary at the time.

September 5

I used to have very bad teeth, in reality. I would pack bits of napkin into the holes between them. In my dream the packing in my teeth was always coming out. I always had to mess with that packing. I awoke.

September 6

My husband and I were at a party. It was a big party; there were lots of people there. There were a lot of rooms between the barn and the house. We walked around every bit of it. Some sections had been recently worked on and some sections were old and crumbling. All of it was cluttered. As we were wandering, I noticed my husband had caught the eye of another woman. She had dark hair and a couple of kids. After eye contact, he started suggesting that I look tired and maybe I should go home. I started walking down the road toward home. Then I decided to turn around and go back. When I got there, I quietly walked in and started looking for my husband. I found them in the living room sitting on the floor. That dark-haired woman was on the floor next to him. They had their heads together talking, just as close as could be and very lovingly. The kids were all over my husband. I walked right up in front of them. They didn't see me because they were so involved with each other. I kicked them both right in the face, turned around and left. I awoke.

September 9

Inside a large building, a parade was going to occur. Two dozen elephants, of all sizes, were lining up. An elephant fight started! The people on the elephant's backs couldn't control them. Trunks were swinging and slapping. Big elephants were pounding the backs of little ones. Screams of people and elephants filled the air. It was awful! I ran out of the building as quick as I could. I awoke.

September 12

I went to work, for one day, at a factory that was a mixture between Arlington Sample Book and WPI. I had worked there before. I took Puppa with me. At first people were upset. They were upset that I was back, I addressed that right away. I said," Hi" to my friends, and then said to the others, "you're just pissed because I was faster and more accurate than you. You're jealous of my more production". Then someone complained about Puppa. I said, "Okay I can solve this and put his service dog patch on him. Then no one could say anything". I was working along and cleaning the place up. I walked past the Vice President, Bob N. and he asked me to come into his office, I did with Puppa. He said, "I want to give you a Bull Terrier". I looked in the next room and there was a cute Bull Terrier, gray, pup. It was dragging its ass on the floor. I said, "It has worms, but I'll take it". There were other bull terriers there, they all had worms.

For some reason Puppa became two Puppas, one was blonde and the other was black. I tried to get the two dogs to become one again: by colliding them, it didn't work. I ran around all day with one. A guy came up to me and wanted to see Puppa's ID. I rummaged around in my purse and found Puppa's ID card and told him if he disputes Puppa's service, he could call the American Disabilities and Justice Department. It wouldn't bother me. I'd already won a case with Hannaford's with the Justice Department. Then I went back to work for my one day. I awoke.

September 13

My husband, granddaughter and I lived in a little cabin. An area to park was across the street. The kitchen sink was a deep one, about four times the size of a regular sink. There was an attached barn. We had a pinto horse and a cow. The house was filthy so my husband and I worked all day cleaning it. It seemed to have a film of white fat or grease on everything. People came over to visit; they seem to be people I went to school with. We went into the barn to see the horse. The horse was dirty too, it needed a bath and brushing. The horse also needed riding. I felt bad that it was in need of attention. When the people left, I cleaned the sink. My granddaughter and I got in the sink for a bath. The two of us just fit. I could see out the window across from the sink. A group of beautiful vehicles came to our parking place. The vehicles were like motorcycles but were something different. They were something I'd never seen before. They were beautifully painted and all glossy. I was surprised that they were parked in our area; I thought they were just driving through on the road. I didn't have time to get out of our bath. So I just curled in a ball, so no parts would be seen. When the people came in they saw my granddaughter and I in the sink. They kind of looked in the sink as they walked by to visit with my husband. I awoke.

September 17

My husband, his sister, her son, my granddaughter and I were living in an apartment in the city. I came home one day and found many things in the apartment that were not mine. I noticed blood, small amounts, on our bed. There were kitchen utensils that were not mine. I asked my husband what was going on. He said they were his girlfriend's, Hope Harmony. I asked about the blood. He said it was from her, they had had sex on the bed during her time a month. There were about four dinners on the counter, mostly veggie meals (one of cabbage). I threw them in the trash. My husband sat at the table grinning not saying a word. Then I started going through the kitchen utensils one by one. If they were not familiar I threw them out. I hit my husband with a wooden spoon. He just smiled, knowing they were hers. I said give me all your cash, and he did. I hid it in the bedroom. I spoke with his sister in the bathroom. She did not know that my husband and I had been together for 23 years. I told them all to pack up and leave. My husband had no problem with this. I got the money out of hiding and put the money in my pocket. I went for a taxi ride which took me through a park. I spoke with the driver during the trip, he was sympathetic with me. I thanked him for his kindness and words of wisdom. He thanked me back for the thank you. When I got back home the bedroom had been rearranged. Most things were packed up. I wanted to go through the stuff my husband had packed, knowing that most of the stuff in the apartment I owned. I awoke.

Note: My husband doesn't have a sister.

September 18

I was working in a restaurant. I came into work and started doing some dishes, in one of the sinks. I didn't get very far before I realized I had to go pee. I looked around for the bathroom. When I found one, I opened the door and there was a little short potty for kids. I hiked up my dress to squat on it and Randy Quade popped his head in and started laughing at me. I was embarrassed and jumped up. I went looking for an adult bathroom. I went out of the restaurant and down a hallway. The floor was like a woven floor, like a mat. I walked on until I found a blanket over a doorway, there was a toilet there. I sat down to pee. All of a sudden the curtain lifted and there were two china men looking at me. They were hanging on the rail of the porch outside the bathroom. I was shocked! I wondered what they were doing. Then I saw a parade going by. A king or emperor was going by. He was sitting on a hand carried bed. Everyone behind him was on more little beds with wheels. They were lying on their stomachs and paddling down the road, they had to keep their heads lower than the emperors. I went back to the restaurant. While walking back, I noticed the woven floor had many holes in it; that people could fall through. I got back into the restaurant and headed to the first of the three sinks. I was surprised to find in the sinks were a bunch of boxes, in the water. I was wondering what was going on. The woman, who ran the restaurant, came over to me and pointed to some stacked Tupperware that had UPC codes on them. She was soaking the boxes to get the UPC's off. I started getting them off. I awoke.

September 24 – Dream #1

Someone like Sean Connery was chasing a monkey, a cute little monkey. Sean Connery finally caught him with a rope. He wanted to eat the monkey. We were indoors. A fire was built; Sean Connery threw the rope, with the monkey tied to it over a hook. The monkey was still alive! The hook was over the fire. The monkey suffered and writhed over the fire until dead!

Dream #2

I had moved in with Eric and Jezebel. The house was a beautiful one, I think it had been redone. The stairs were oak platforms. It was pouring rain one night and the cattle were in the field. One of the dogs, a female, was out and wouldn't come back in. We went to our rooms and went to bed. The next morning the stairs were all wet from footprints. I went to get a mop, there were four in the closet: one nub, one small one, and my 2 mops that had full mop heads. I grabbed a mop of mine and went to sop up the water, on the stairs. I looked out the window and saw the dog tormenting the Herford cattle. All of a sudden a longhorn Herford stomped the dog! I hollered, "That's it! The cattle got her". Eric and Jezebel went running out to the scene. I went to the garden; there were three, tumbleweed like, balls there. The balls were originally animals; I changed them into the tumbleweeds. The animals had been dying so

I changed them. That way they could be taken care of at a later time. I was awoken by my husband.

September 28

I went to see Little Man, (the white Arabian horse I had as a teenager- in real life). He was staying at the Inn at Danbury with Alex and Bob G. There were a couple of other horses there. Little man was the best of the bunch. Some men were there to clean out the barn. Bob and gotten out of the inn business, and was dealing in surplus and antiques now. His daughters had moved out, his son stayed home. I wanted to ride Little Man, but couldn't find his saddle and bridle. I asked Bob where they were, he had no idea. He asked me, "what kind of saddle"? I replied, "English hunt". He said, "Hmmm, I've not seen an English saddle at all". I said, "well- Carolyn must have put it somewhere. I had been letting Carolyn ride whenever she wanted to". I led little man around by his mane looking for the saddle. The workers were mad at Alex. She kept getting them up in the middle of the night to start working. They saw no reason for this. Bob was on the porch sitting on a friendly brown horse, talking to his workers. I asked him again about the saddle and bridle. He hadn't seen it. My husband woke me up.

September 30

I was in the hospital. Nobody could figure out what was wrong with me. I kept having episodes. One night my husband came into my room. He said he was going to stay with me, for the night. He said it would help avoid an episode. I asked him how. He told me this story – "a bear comes into your room each night, he is invisible at first. Then he takes solid shape and frightens you. When you get scared the bear attacks and mauls you. In the future people will talk with their hands". I replied, "What the hell! How did you come up with that"? "After each episode, you tell the doctors a little bit about what has happened. They finally pieced it all together". Then a hospital bed begins to rise. I'm getting scared. My husband tells me, "keep cool, don't be scared, ignore it, it's the bear". The bed rises 20 feet and I'm freaking out. My husband says," don't be scared, calm down". The bear materializes, comes over and sniffs me. I reach out and touch it. It roams around the room for a while. I watch it, trying not to show fear. Our Great Dane was there. The bear grabbed our dog. He took Cochise into a chamber, like a box which was half full of fluid. That bear started having anal sex with our dog! Afterwards the bear came out of the chamber. He got a fork and a knife and went back into the chamber and ate our dog! I awoke.

October 1

Me and three girlfriends were going to go see some friends. To see them we had to walk through a long tunnel underground. Things started out fine – we were happy and chatting. We stopped for a break, and spoke of how good it will be to see our friends. As we got further into the tunnel, we notice sinister people in the shadows. We quickened our pace. Then people started chasing us. These people had razor blades that were like five sided field point arrow tips. One sinister person; let's call them zombies now, because they wanted to kill us, slashed me across the left shoulder. I was bleeding but didn't stop to see how badly. Throughout the tunnel zombies were slashing away at us. One zombie man got real close to me. He slashed my other shoulder, my head and legs. I kicked him in the balls many times. Finally, he doubled over and I took his razor blades away from him. I started slashing zombies back and running. At some point our group was down to just two of us. We couldn't stop or we'd die. There was a family, with a little girl, at an intersection. The parents were bleeding all over – they were done. They asked us to please take their child, to save her. I grabbed her up and ran down the left side of the tunnel. Every time a zombie came close to me I'd slash them with the stolen blade. Each time I use the blade one of its pointed edges came off. I was down to my last single blade. I saw Kenny G. in the tunnel. I didn't know if I should trust him or if he was zombie. He said, "Follow me. I'll help you get out of here, and I did. He ran interference for us. We made it out of the tunnel. We crouched down at the edge to see what was beyond. A river ran by, going the other way. A concrete ledge was there before the river. There were zombies below the ledge and bodies in the river. It was all so gross. We snuck around the ledge to a field. There were zombies in the field and woods around us. At some point, I think I lost the child. We were down to just two of us. We snuck through the grass and bushes on high alert. Finally, we saw a dump truck hauling a load of dirt. It was a very large truck. We ran up to it, climbed inside the back, to get a ride away. There were others, who had escaped, doing the same thing. We were all bleeding very badly, but we were safe. At some point, when I felt we were far enough away, I slid out the back of the truck – grateful to be alive. I awoke my shoulders are killing me.

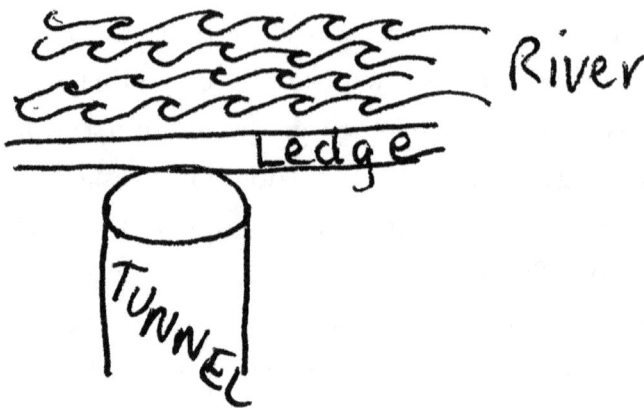

October 12

I was in school, a boarding school. One weekend when the school was empty, a group of people came to the school. They were vaccinating babies. They were staying for the weekend at the school. My room – which had bunk beds, was the first room as you came into the dorm area. So a pair of older ladies came into my room. I told them they could stay but the bottom bunk was my bed. I went to watch the guy giving shots to the babies. He started out with Saran wrap on his hands and that didn't work well. I went and got him a cup full of doctor style gloves that were in the cupboard of medical supplies. He thanked me. I watched him for a long time. He got angry with me. He turned on me and shouted, "Why are you watching me? Do you think I'm doing something wrong"? I was shocked at this. I replied, "No, I think it's amazing that not one of the babies you have vaccinated has cried". I smiled and walked away.

I went into one of the three gyms on campus. I opened the gym door and there was a black man sitting on the floor. He asked if I could help him up because he was drunk. I did. I turned and noticed a lot of people in the gym. The people were line dancing to pop rock funk music. I tried to do it but couldn't keep up. I moved into the next gym. There were people doing the same thing but better. I left. As I was going out the door an animal ran inside. It was red and I thought it was a fox. I grabbed it and put it back outside. I took a good look at it and saw that it was a Pomeranian type dog with a sweater on. The sweater was handmade red and blue. I started patting the dog and it rolled over on its side, happy. I woke.

October 13

My granddaughter and I were living in a more populated area of a town. She was taking a nap. I looked out the window in her room and thought I saw something. I kept looking and some tree branches moved. It was a moose. The antlers I thought were branches. I went to other windows in the house – the moose was still there. I noticed a cow moose also; she was light-colored blonde/red. A bit of woods was a buffer near a row of homes. I snuck out with a camera. I got in a great place for a photo. As soon as I lifted the camera for a shot the two moose ran off. Next I knew I was walking with my Mom on a road, telling her about it. I awoke. I fell back asleep.

Dream #2

I was visiting Michelle C. I remember really wanting to chug down a half gallon of cranberry juice. I was babysitting for her. She had left a message with me, for her dad. When he got home, I was to ask him if he had any EEE (triple E) mosquito killer. Michelle had wanted to spread it around her house. I thought it would be too strong with a baby around, but this was in my head. After a while, Michelle's dad came home. He looked in the refrigerator said, "what's this"? As he grabbed out a jug of 12 days old apple cider, I had brought with me. I told him it was 12-day-old apple cider. He got a big glass out of a cabinet and started drinking it all. Afterwards, he lit up a joint and offered me some. I took a hit! It was so strong. It made me so high I couldn't speak! I tried many times to tell him the message from Michelle. I couldn't get the words out. I had to write it to him. I went home.

Dream #3

My husband and I were outside having a pit fire in the snow. Puppa was with us as well as my daughter. My daughter was still in high school. She came home with a new pair of shoes on, tall sandals like pumps and brown. She had a black skirt on with an empire waist shirt. I asked her where she got the shoes. She answered her boyfriend. I looked her up and down and asked her if she was pregnant. We walked over by the house and she told me that she was! At the edge of the woods I could see dogs jumping over the stonewall – I thought they were coyotes. I tried to holler to my husband, "coyotes"! Eventually the words came out. He fired his gun at one, and hit it. The dogs still came, about 8 to 10 of them. They worked as a pack/team trying to go after Puppa. I kept screaming. The dogs were someone's dogsled team and not coyotes. I grabbed Puppa and went back over to my daughter. I asked her how far along she was. We both thought it was time to abort her pregnancy. I asked her about her boyfriend, which I didn't know she had. She stated she liked to have sex on a beaver blanket, the hairs tickled her ass. I went back over near the fire. There was blood from the dog that my husband shot. It was going to live. The pack worked its way across the street. I awoke.

October 15

A girlfriend, (Sue or Jill- I don't know which) and I got a hotel room in a small hotel. We had one of the two large rooms in the building. We also had Carl P stay with us??? We were waiting for my granddaughter to arrive. There were no beds. We brought our own blankets and made our nests on the floor. Carl went out for a while. My granddaughter hadn't arrived yet. Carl came in with a blanket over his shoulder like a Santa Claus sack. He dumped out his blanket laughed and left. Smart ass he had emptied into the room hundreds of swamp creatures! Oh my God what a mess! All our blankets were wet and crawling. My friend and I started trying to catch everything and get it out of the room. There were fish, lizards, bugs, and leeches. We worked frantically to try and clear the room before my granddaughter arrived. I went to see if there was another room available to stay in, no vacancy. We grabbed catfish, big lizards and small, throwing out bugs, scooping up stuff as fast as possible. At one point, I stopped, feeling something. I opened my mouth and a large tadpole looking leech was stuck to my tongue. I had to peel it off. I was so mad at Carl P.

Note: No frogs or snakes, no symbols of change. Must've been Susie – Jill would've made Carl clean the mess.

October 18

Note: first night of new medication – having hard time recalling dream.

Austin Powers and I bought a restaurant in the city. It was run down, but I liked that run down theme. We ripped a few things out and made it even more " hole in the wall". We were having fun. We were going around checking everything out, making everything dumpy and hillbilly. I noticed a wall that was like a pocket door. I opened the wall and behind it was a church stairway. The stairway was covered in blue foam. At the top of the stairs, right behind the door, was a dead baby held tight blue foam! I went back to my hotel room – which had a plain square key. Austin was there and was very excited about the new business venture. He had all kinds of ideas about costumes for the staff, dresses from curtains etc. We went to a model show of clothes for restaurants. Every model and uniform was beautiful. We wanted our waitresses clothing line to be shown also. We asked if we could join in. They said yes. Some of the hotel help, where the show was, just got off work. They were fat and dumpy. We asked them if they would help us with our fashion line. They agreed. We left that hotel, which had a fancy key, to go to our hotel to get the curtains and stuff that we had been playing with. Once out on the street I couldn't think of where our hotel was. I examined the keys for a clue, but mine was plain and square. Didn't know where to go.

Note: During dream, I spoke aloud and my husband heard me.

October 23

I went somewhere that had a gym floor. I was staying for a few nights and had a dorm room with some of the girls. I love the gym floor. I found I could skate without skates, just using my own shoes. I skated all the time. Figure eights, circles, arcs front and back, all I wanted to do was skate. I had no wheels on my shoes. The girls in my room were ready to leave. I asked them to pack my stuff and double check to make sure nothing was left behind. I skated. It was time to leave. I had to be kicked out, I just wanted to skate. I awoke.

END OF VOLUME 3

VOLUME 4

October 25

I was at a resort somewhere. I didn't have a room there, I was just visiting. I felt like I was crashing the place like a wedding. I ate at a large food buffet, just picking at foods as I looked around. I was exploring the whole place. In one area was a flea market. I looked around and found a ceramic Mother Goose that I had made. It was about a foot tall. I had sold it in previous years, when needing money. I was so surprised to see it there. It took all of my money to buy it back. A woman offered me a ride home and I accepted. We were in her car getting ready to go, the window was down. A man came up to the window, drew out a sword and cut off her arm. I just looked at my goose and admired my work. The goose's wing was beautifully painted, with a one-stroke glaze that was somewhat transparent in each feather. The feathers were swirly and I was proud. I felt, if I didn't look at the crime being committed, the guy wouldn't come after me. I was so scared. The man left. I looked over the goose again and the head fell off! I got out of the car and snuck away, upset over the goose and the crime. I didn't want the man to see me and come after me. I went back into the resort. There were two doors side-by-side, (might've been a French door). One door said," day", in French, the other said, "night", in French. I wondered what that was about. I thought maybe one was for man and one was for women. I went into the day door. Within were lounges, corners of light and dark, a swimming pool, tables and chairs. There was a family in the pool with a small child. The child was standing on the father's hand. There were many people sitting poolside. I sat down to watch the people in and around the pool. A butch blonde woman came and sat next to me. She leaned over and whispered in my ear. I didn't move. She basically said to me, "meet me in my room. I'm in room number one. I want to have my way with you. If you don't come to my room I'll hunt you down. So you better do as I say". I kept quiet while she spoke to me. She got up and walked out. I looked beyond where she had been sitting, at another woman. She made eye contact with me and started shaking her head- no. I was a bit scared. I looked down, the butch had left behind a large change purse. I opened it and it was full of money, I saw a 50 dollar bill and knew there was a lot of money in there. I closed the purse and got up to leave, taking the purse with me. I didn't go to the woman's room. I took the purse and left the resort. I went to train station. I wanted to go home. I didn't want to be around the sex and violence at the resort. I had stolen the purse and was afraid of being caught with it. In the train station were lots of plants. I had to pick my way through the plants to get to the train. I awoke.

October 30

I was at work one day, a woman came up to me and said," I'm your sister". I replied, "Like hell". She said, "Our Mom had me out of wedlock and put me up for adoption". I just stood there with my mouth hanging open, like an idiot. All this news came the day after a fire had damaged mom and dad's house. The fire had consumed a whole exterior wall. I went to Mom and Dad's house to talk to them. The place was boarded up and looked like a haunted house at a carnival. A note was on the boards saying we have moved to... Address. I went to the new address, Mom and Dad were there. I asked Mom about the sister thing. That sister was there! She had moved in with them! I was angry about the whole thing. Mom hung her head with guilt and said, "Yes this happened. She is your sister". I looked around the place and asked, "What are you guys doing here"? "We bought this house and are going to live here". I asked, "How can you do this"? Mom replied, "We did a reverse mortgage before the fire. With the money we bought this house and we're not going back". I looked around, there were only two bedrooms, one for my parents and the other had four beds and it; two for my brothers and two for me and the new sister. I saw this and said, "no way – like hell. Can I have the old house"? They said, "Sure we're not doing anything with it". I went to the old home and looked around. The wall in the kitchen was gone but could be replaced. Pets were still there, cat and a horse??? I awoke

Note: My parent's house was actually destroyed by fire years ago. They rebuilt on the same site.

November 4

My husband, I, Cheryl and my granddaughter moved into a wicked large house. My husband and I were not doing so great. He had a family reunion to go to, I didn't attend. Cheryl, my granddaughter and I were exploring the house. We thought we were in one room and we discovered we were in one wing. There was a live-in helper just for our wing. The place came furnished. The decor had little to be desired. Every surface was covered with knickknacks. Mostly fish, poor quality ones. The dining room had nice tables, there were four of them, two round and two rectangular. The live-in help had his own suite of rooms. We explored everything. There were photos on the shelf of the live-in help's bedroom. I picked up the photos, there were a set of three. My daughter was in the photos with another girl. I showed them to Cheryl. She says, "that's Sam"! I said, "and my daughter"! The photos was taken at a house at a party. I didn't want to be there. I thought we should leave and live somewhere else. I kept looking around the house. My mind was starting to change about leaving. We took a walk and found a beautiful white beach. In the water were neon tetra's, they were so beautiful against the white beach sand. I had socks on and went into the water wading. I looked at the fish from different angles. When I went to get out of the water, I noticed it was not beach sand. It was white crystals and could eat up your feet. I hopped over the beach area. Then warned Cheryl of the glass like crystals. I awoke.

November 6

My brother was here from Alaska, I believe it was for a holiday. I was riding a bicycle through New London. I had been smoking a joint. (???) The asphalt turned to concrete just before the gallery area. The concrete looked fresh and wet to me. A cop car was sitting there in a lane that narrowed down. As I was passing by I noticed a sawhorse roadblock. I had to stop my bike. A lady cop got out of her patrol car and said, "we are stopping you because these sensors, and she pointed to a strip along the car side panel trim, went off detecting marijuana. You'll have to come with me". The sensor read a level of 1.5, which was way over the limit. I went with her to the police station, she wrote up the paperwork. My brother showed up to help me. The lady cop was so nice, a few of my friends were her friends. The lady cop showed me a fish tank she was cleaning, it contained neon tetras and other tetras. We spoke of them. I left the station thinking about ways to beat the rap. My brother went out to the parking lot, stood there and scratched his head. He couldn't find the car he came in. I awoke.

November 11

My granddaughter and I were staying at a home on top of the mountain. A nice high mountain like the White Mountains. There was a rocky knob just outside the house where people would come to sightsee. I had a lot of money about $16,000 on me. A couple of guys, that look like lucky on the King of the Hill TV show, where there. For some reason I trusted them. I had my granddaughter in a baby stroller on the knob looking at the view. My purse was hanging off the back of the stroller. Those two guys offered to push my granddaughter around for me. I didn't think anything about it, and allowed it. They had a grocery bag that they hung beside my purse. As we were walking around they kept getting into my purse, stealing my money and putting it into their bag. A boy in the house noticed the men stealing from me. The boy came out of the house and told me I was being robbed. I turned around and grabbed both bags and confronted the two men. They ran off. I emptied their bag and found $8000 and some drugs. I kicked myself for not asking them to empty their pockets. They got away with half my money. I awoke to pee.

Dream #2 – Hard to Recall

I was outside, somewhere, picking veggies. Drew Barrymore stopped by! She was just passing by and stopped. She spent the day with us. We were excited and amazed. To leave my garden you had to walk over the roof of a barn. The roof was in bad shape and wooden. You could see the joists, in between sagged. I stepped with an arm load of tomatoes and fell through the roof. I was okay. As night came we went into the barn. A reggae singer was there. He sang a song and we danced. The barn door opened and the rest of his bands came in. The group set up and we danced the night away. Drew was wearing a pair of shoes much like mine with rounded toes. Hers where Olive Oil style – chunky shoes. I awoke.

November 12

I rented a flat in a building that I had been in 20 years earlier. I was on the second floor this time, having rented the first floor before. I started an advertisement business. I put in a front desk and had some tables put around. I hired a woman to man the front desk. She was young, single and a brunette. We opened and were flooded with male customers. We serve drinks while the businessmen waited. I went around to each man to see what they wanted for ads. I had a machine that produced the advertisements. The ads looked funny – little cutouts like pixels on paper. These would be fed through another machine to be inked and printed. I had a hard time seeing the original master ads. The ads would distort when held up due to all the cutouts. I tried putting a piece of paper behind them to make it more rigid and visible. I finally made it through all the customers.

Whew! I went up to my front desk secretary saying, "this isn't going to work this way". She thought I was getting rid of her. I asked her if we could switch positions. I would be front desk and she would handle the ad customers. She was elated and gave me a hug. I couldn't see the ads well enough to continue doing that part of the job. A man came down from upstairs, he had a clipboard. He asked me if he'd seen me before – I told him that I had rented from him 20 years ago. He walked off with a smile. I stood back and looked around. The walls were only painted halfway up. The walls were so tall. I'd have to get someone in with scaffolding to paint. I awoke.

November 16 – Nap

My husband wanted me to do something bookkeeping related. I went to a room on the second or third floor, to my desk. I noticed the bottom of the window was missing and that the glass of been chewed away. I had a window box outside and the whole front of the window box was gone. The dirt was falling out. A huge squirrel was gnawing away everything. I tried to scare him away, but it didn't work. I yelled for my husband. He came into the room and looked at the squirrel. The damn thing was the size of the small cat. The squirrel wasn't afraid. The squirrel came into the room. I was having an ADHD moment. I noticed there were Christmas decorations and a small tree up. I thought- what the hell. Why didn't I clean up this room earlier? I started to pick up while my husband chased the squirrel. There were party supplies all over. I started to pack them up. My husband wanted me to do the office work. I found a little party Queen crown in a package, and put it on my granddaughter.

Then I noticed it had snowed out and wondered why my husband wasn't deer hunting.

Dream Switched

I was in our old blue pickup truck. There were no brakes. I stood on the brakes, I jumped up and down to try and get them to work. I wanted to try and get a food basket, we had no food. The woman handing out the food baskets ignored me. I was very upset. I drove to New London. I saw a large long box on the side of the road. I went past it trying to stop. I had to swing around and go back to stop. I got out, hoping there was food in it – the box contained clothes and such. I knew a college student had it fall out of the back of their truck. A food woman stopped to look the box over too. I told her that I had hoped there was food in it. She just started going through the clothes and feeling lucky. I told her that the person who lost it would be back for it. She just pawed through things. She wanted to keep everything. As she was pawing through a truck pulled up, the owner had retraced their steps to get their box. I awoke when my husband came in the room.

November 23

I was in college, I guess, living in a dorm room with another woman. One day I met Brandon Frazier. He was living in another dorm room! He started flirting with me. It didn't take long to have my attention, hook line and sinker. Over time I went to his room – he had roommates. I tried to keep very discreet with our visits. Rumors started going around with the men and women of the dorms. I tried to tell folks we were just friends, they wouldn't believe me. Brandon wanted me!! I wouldn't let him have me. I was married. I really wanted a tryst with Brandon but my morals wouldn't allow it. Brandon kept at me – romancing, touching, and wearing me down. One day he kissed me! He wanted to French kiss, me but I wouldn't allow it. My dentures and being inhibited wouldn't allow it. I tried to explain to him. He was bummed out but still kept after me. His roommate was always coming in and catching us in closeness. Rumors were flying. Boy, I wanted him, –the thought of my husband still held me back, but I was weakening. Brandon got his own room. I visited him. He was rubbing up against me; he wanted me to take my clothes off. I was so inhibited. I said, "Why do you want to see a 50-year-old, heavy woman nude"? I couldn't bring myself to do it. I showed him my tattoos – he wanted it all. l Weird! Posey knocked on the door and woke me.

November 27

We were on a walk about. There was my husband and some other people with me. We each had a suitcase with the things we needed. We would walk as far as we could in a day and camp at night. We went as far north as we were comfortable with, then headed south. All just for the heck of it. One night we stopped near a house to camp. Through the windows, I could see a child with downs syndrome. He was playing in a room all by himself. In the morning Aunt Sandy came to the house. I was surprised! The child was her grandchild. The next thing I knew the room with the downs child started flooding with water. The child had broken a pipe. What a mess. We left. I had left my suitcase behind and only had a plastic bag. We continued to head south. As we were going along the scenery changed. Beside the road puddles of water laced the area. It was beautiful with the pockets of water dotted all along the way. As we continued, the puddles got deeper and larger. The water was so clear. Along the way there was a young man fishing. He asked us; "Can you see any fish?" A monster fish was just behind him. I shouted to him about it. He cast his line near it and the fish was right on his bait. The fish was huge. The man was happy he landed the fish. He invited us to his house, just back a few hundred feet. We walked down the driveway with him. As we walked, water came in and covered the driveway – almost like a tide. We had to stay until the water receded. We were allowed to stay in the house. The owners of the house, (a Mom and Dad) were speaking to us in the living room. I lit a joint?? I held it cupped in my hand. The young man, son, smelled it and wanted some. He suggested we go outside with it. We walked outside the house onto a path. The path led us to a beautifully arched wooden bridge. As I was walking over the bridge with him I noticed a pygmy hippopotamus in the water under the bridge. I was amazed. I pointed it out to the man as I passed the joint to him. He smiled and said, "Yeah, we have 17 of them that live under the bridge". I looked harder and saw couple more lying on the river bottom. I woke.

November 28

My husband and I rented an apartment on the second floor of a brick townhouse. It was comfortable, but I didn't like the landlord much. For some reason we had our laundry sent out to be done. When it would come back, it was packed in plastic bags that looked like space savers. I started noticing baby creatures running around our apartment: ducks, frogs, lizards, chickens. All these things came from eggs. We had to watch our step around the apartment, there were so many things running around. I tried to figure out what everything needed to eat. More creatures appeared. One day, I noticed there were eggs in our clean bag of laundry. So weird. By then there were beautiful chameleons and nasty Komodo dragons. Our place was crawling with creatures. I even saw a baby raccoon one day. I stopped sending the laundry out. I decided to do the laundry in the basement myself. The stairs were narrow stone steps. At the bottom was a large round table that a lot of men sat at. I think they were playing cards. When I was ready to go upstairs with my laundry, the men all stopped and stared at me. I was wearing a dress and no underwear. They were waiting for a peep show. I tried to gather my dress and go discreetly. The stairs were too narrow. Two other women, in pants, tried to get me moving – I kicked them down. I was upset. The men got their show. I awoke.

November 29

For some reason, my husband and I lost our house. We had a strong, solid house (the one we live in now). We had to move into a very old, weak house. My son was with us. There were two bedrooms downstairs, then a second floor with two or more bedrooms. My husband and I had a bedroom on the first floor. My son had a first floor bedroom that was only large enough for a bed. My son also had the upstairs. The stairs leading to the upstairs were terrible, they were narrow and rickety. A friend of my son's came by one day. I gave him a tour of the house. There was a hole in the middle of the kitchen floor, where my husband was doing some repairs. I took the friend of my son's upstairs. Puppa went with us. We went up the flight of stairs, it made a left-hand turn. At the turn there was no rail or banister. I thought Puppa would fall through; it was such a narrow way. As I was going up, to show this area, I was thinking of how to change the stair to make it more sturdy and functional – maybe a few stairs, a platform and more stairs, or widen the staircase or something. I awoke. The dog needed to go out.

December 6

Suzie and I were housemaids in a rented home. There were a group of people renting the house; one of the people was Johnny Depp. I was so thrilled to be able to see him and on a regular basis. Every once in a while he'd say to me, "you know what I want?" I'd hand him a joint. He'd smile and wander off to go smoke. Nobody else in the group smoked. The kitchen was large and old-fashioned. Suzy and I would serve the group meals at a large long table. We did the cooking and the cleanup. When it was time for the group to leave the rental, we waved goodbye. I was bummed to say goodbye to Johnny. We went back into the house to clean up the kitchen. The counters were covered with stuff. The sink was full of dishes. Suzy was doing dishes and was trying to clean the counters and the refrigerator. I put some leftovers in the trash, one left over we took home with us. It was a desert: a lemon curd with little pinched square pastries, about an inch square. I got all the trash off the counter. We get the dishes done. Suzy wanted to leave. There were still things on the counter, a lot of hinges. The hinges were scattered all over the kitchen. I gathered them into a pile, there were 11 pair. I didn't know what to do with them, so I put them in a drawer. Finally the counter was clean and we could leave. I awoke.

December 8

My husband and I went to a lake. There we met a woman with a Rottweiler dog. The dog was swimming in the water with the woman. When we arrived, she put the dog in a wooden cage. The cage had chicken wire windows and was on legs, much like Jill's chicken coop only larger. The dog pen was in the water. I swam out a ways beyond the cage. The dog looked at me through the cage back window. My husband stayed and talked with the woman. All of a sudden the woman picked up the cage, dog and all, and threw it into her convertible car. She and my husband drove off! By the time I got out of the water my husband was waving goodbye. Puppa and I walked to a mall type place and went in. We walked around; I was looking for a telephone. I needed a ride home. All of a sudden people started running by in a panic. I lost Puppa in the stampede! I was frantic calling for him. I ran into a restaurant looking for him. I asked a waitress what was going on. She said, there was a vampire here. I went out into the hall calling for Puppa. The woman came up to me and said, "Here's your dog". That dog was small and black, but not Puppa. She gave the dog to me. I said, "This isn't Puppa". She said, "Well let's go outside and leave the door open. You call your dog, we'll see if he comes out", I agreed. We went outside, left the doors open and called. Many dogs came out. All sizes most were black. None were Puppa. The woman asked me if she could do anything for me. I said, "I need a ride home." She said, "no problem my truck is right over there." She pointed to a brown pickup. We got in – I was so sad, no Puppa and my husband run off with another woman. She started driving me home. At some point I noticed we were not going to my house. We were on the wrong road. I hollered, "Stop! This is not the way". She stopped. I knew at that point that she was the vampire. I was pleading with her to not do this to me. She got me out of the truck and lifted me up so I was facing her. I pleaded more. I looked into her eyes, beautiful blue swirls and I melted. I felt so sexually attracted to her. She was carrying me to a house across the way. I started telling her how I'd be hers if she didn't bite me. I told her how she made me melt, when I looked into her eyes. We got to the house and there was a man lugging in wood there. The woman took me inside. The man came in with the wood. I asked him if I could stay. He couldn't answer me, his words were all garbled. The woman asked him if she could keep me. The man started to answer when I saw the problem to his speech. He didn't have a tongue but a mouthful of tentacles. I knew he was a vampire to. I awoke before I got the answer.

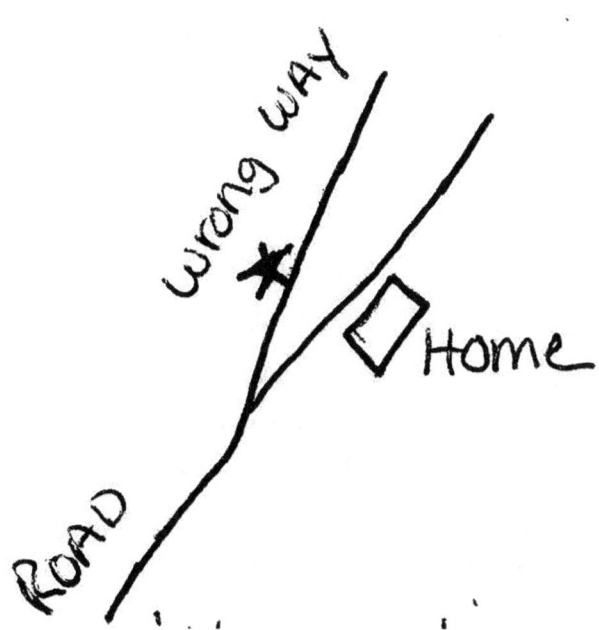

December 13 – Nap

My husband came into the house. He asked me, "Why did you act so during the power outage"? I told him, "Because I am a caregiver. It's my job to tend to things here at the house". My husband started taking down the coats on the living room coat rack. I asked him. "What you're looking for"? He replied, "The ring I gave you". I looked at him like he was crazy. I replied, "That burned in the house fire. So who is she? I know you've met someone". He looked at me like he was on the fence deciding to say or not. I said come on; I know you've been with someone for a while. My husband replied, "Melissa Atkinson". I asked who she was and he said, "a teacher at Proctor". I slapped his face hard. I was going to punch him in the face but didn't, "you're not worth it", I said. At this point he got out some grocery bags, (Brown paper) and started filling his bags with things from the pantry. I told him, "take vegetables and things my granddaughter and I won't eat and get to hell out". Then I noticed there were cooked egg noodles all around the refrigerator. They were on top of it and behind it as well. I said, "What to hell"! As my husband was leaving, I reminded him to leave his key.

Dream #2

Puppa and I went to visit Jezebel and Eric, at Battle's farm. I was smoking a cigarette inside a breezeway (that doesn't really exist). When I finished it, I went outside to put it out. Then I went into the house to see them. I asked, "What you guys doing here?" They looked at me and smiled. I never got an answer to my question. We smoked and I left. I went home to bed. I was all snuggled in and warm when there was a knock on the door. I hollered, "Come in". Eric and Jezebel came in and jumped on my bed. They were in a great mood. I noticed Jezebel had cute little teeth (weird). They stayed for a while then left.

January 2

My husband, my son, my granddaughter, Puppa and I went camping. I want to say we were at Kezar Lake. Hank and Helga ran the campground. We chose the site near the hot tub. The hot tub was like a child's wading pool. The tub near our campsite was not ready for use. It needed cleaning – there was a lot of sand and debris in it. We cleaned it out and refilled it. I knew it wouldn't be ready until the next day. We were bummed. We drove down the road a little bit. There was an observation cabin by a river. Inside the cabin was another hot tub. There were two doors: one at road level and one at river bank level. We were getting in the hot tub when the lower door opened. The oxy clean guy and his dog came in. This guy was the caretaker of the cabin. He told his dog to leave us alone; Puppa was a little bit nasty. He said, "Hi", and then left. I awoke – my husband said he could hear coyotes on the other side of the road.

January 6

My husband and I were not doing well. He had his eyes on someone else. There was no communication. One day he said, "We're done. I have a girlfriend". He wanted me to move out of the bedroom into another. I didn't want to. I thought he should move into the other room. Because we couldn't talk to each other, I went into the other bedroom. I was angry. I wanted my bed. I went out for walk. It was winter. I just wandered around thinking. Mattie was out plowing. He saw me and pulled over. He asked what I was doing. I told him my husband and I broke up and that I was just walking around. He said, "Get in the truck and come with me". We went to a casual home type bar. I started my period! I was unprepared – it had been a long time since I had had my period. Dave S. was there also, we sat around visiting. There was another woman there. She had a big butt. She was picking up, straightening up. She was with Mattie, I guess. Dave kept talking to me, visiting, he made me feel better. I went home, told my husband that I wanted my bedroom and that he could move into the other room. I was assertive about it. I was awoken by my husband saying it's 7 o'clock.

January 9

I had a little one-bedroom apartment downtown somewhere. I had little furniture – like a drop leaf table. The building had a revolving front door. I went somewhere for a celebration for mom – maybe a birthday. There were lots of gifts from her. I had nothing so I tried to make her quilt. I didn't do very well with it and got very frustrated. (Not straight and ripped, small, no backing). I tried to go home but wasn't sure where I lived. I let myself go on autopilot. I ended up outside the building with a revolving door. As I got there a couple of young women were outside just around the corner. As I approach the called me over to them. They said, "sshhhh wait –the landlady comes out every day at this time. We can get in when she leaves." These women were homeless and slept in the hallway. They would sneak in as the door revolved, when someone came out. I told them I think I have a key – it was an odd little key. I wasn't sure if it fit that door. The landlady came through the door and the girls rushed in after her, without being seen. I tried my key and it fit, I felt better knowing I lived there. I went on autopilot again to find which apartment was mine. I try the key in the first apartment I came to, it fit! The women came in with me but were looking at me like I didn't know what was going on. I saw their looks and explained to them; I was brain-damaged from having seizures. I told them they could stay at my apartment if they would help me a bit. They agreed and felt themselves to be so lucky. They sat on my couch. I looked outside the window to see the backyard. They also looked around my apartment. They thought it was small. I went to the table and collapse the drop leaf table. This made things a little roomier. On my way back home, I stepped in something. My shoe was all sticky. I went to the women and asked them for help. I lifted my foot and found I'd stepped in honey. The women cleaned off my shoe then followed the trail of honey on the floor. We found five – six honey bears on a low shelf. One of them had fallen over and was dripping on the floor. The women cleaned it up, along with the spots on the floor. The women continue to look around and found I had a TV and a radio system. They felt very lucky and so did I to have their help. I awoke.

January 12

I was playing with my granddaughter. I was saying something to her (the words just left me now). I meant to say the words. My husband heard me and thought I was having an episode. He took me to the hospital. I guess I did pass out or go to sleep. When I awoke I was in a hospital bed. My husband was in the bed next to me. I looked over at him and asked what he was doing there. He said he was going to spend the night with me. A nurse came in and started putting water all over me. I was getting angry, "what to fuck are you doing"? She said she had to keep me wet all night. I said, "Like hell" and got up trying to run off. A little Asian nurse caught up with me and jabbed me with something like Novocain. I went numb and couldn't run anymore. They carried me back to my room. They were going to put me in a bed that had sides, which made the bed look like a trough. There was water in it and shit! Shit was floating all around! I was horrified by the thought of having to be in a bed pool of shit! I said, "What to hell". A nurse exclaimed that I was dehydrated and had bowel problems so this was the answer. I struggled and got away. I started running for an exit. A nurse there locked the door. I ran to another exit – a nurse there locked that door also. I ran in another direction, the whole place was in locked down, to keep me there. A nurse came near me with the Novocain stuff again. I hit her and ran again. Another nurse tried this and I hit her. I was fighting a kicking they finally got me and I awoke.

January 16

My granddaughter and I went to my cousin's house. They were all boys – Brady Bunch type set up. There were four boys varying in age. (I feel this is a reoccurring dream in some way). I have memories of this house. I was hoping to do the laundry and my granddaughter was on her own while I was doing this chore. A nice feather pillow was in the dryer. When it came out of the dryer it was so wonderful. The older boy – who I had a crush on, came into the laundry. I said to him, "Put your face on this". He did and loved it. I took it to his room, on the first floor, and put it on his bed. I took his pillow and put it on another boy's bed upstairs. The boy that owned the feather pillow was upset, he wanted his pillow back. I went to find my granddaughter. She was in the parent's bed room. (I want to say this was Aunt Sandy Uncle Bailey's, but they have no boys). When I got into their room it was trashed! My granddaughter was in there exploring and made a huge mess. Part of the mess was puzzle pieces, all over the floor. The puzzles had been glued together and were standing up on a couch. My granddaughter had wrecked two or three of them. I picked up the puzzle pieces and threw out the puzzles that the pieces had come from. One of the puzzles was a Native American dancer in yellow and red. (It was a puzzle that I really have done and stored it under the couch. I recently threw it out) I picked up toilet paper from all over the floor. The room was a lot better but still a little messy. I gathered my granddaughter up and thought good enough. I went upstairs to one of the boys' bedrooms. The boy said, "Why don't we go downstairs, come on." He opened the door off the living room and went down the stairs. I followed. When we got downstairs there was another living room. I had been there before. I was so happy to be there. I said, "oh yeah I forgot about this". I set my granddaughter down and jumped off the bottom stair and I took such a large leap, I went the whole distance of the room. I floated the last few feet and landed on a semicircle green couch on the other end of the room. I was so happy to be there. My granddaughter was exploring the room. I noticed people outside standing around. There was a window behind the couch. I got on my knees and opened the window. Two of the boys got up beside me. A boy on each side of me. So many people were outside standing around. There were many tables covered in white table cloths. It was a family reunion. As people were arriving the others would clap and say, "hello".

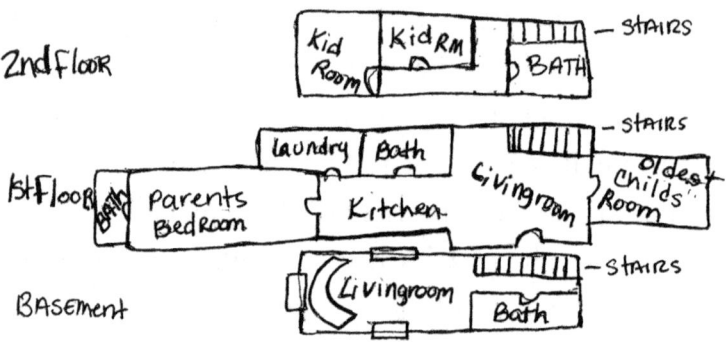

There was a man and his two daughters standing near the open window, I was kneeling at. All of a sudden a big cheer and laughter came from the crowd. I looked and here came a man carrying a canoe with an attached scene, over his head. His family followed him beaming with pride. I said, "I'll be damned, he brought it. Can you believe it"? I was talking to the boys beside me. The man outside turned to me glared. I said, "What the hell"? He said, "your language", pointing to his two girls. I told him," If you don't like it move". He just continued to glare at me. I awoke.

January 17

My husband and I bought a house. I was in a large field with lots of privacy. The field was 5+ acres. Nobody drove the road. There was a house across the way that rarely had anyone in it. One night my husband and I were lying out in the field on a blanket. We fell asleep. At one point in the evening I awoke. I could see headlights coming from an open area by the woods up back. I watched the lights crest the hill, coming toward our house. The vehicle stopped with the lights still on. I could see silhouettes of many people. They were coming down the hill into our field, towards our home. I spoke to my husband, he didn't wake. I raised my voice, still no response. I yelled at my husband and shook him. He woke and saw the people. He pulled out a pistol. We wanted to see what they were going to do. They all came down to the house. There must've been about eight of them. They were at the front of the house when my husband shouted, "that's far enough", from behind them. We were in the dark and in the grass. The group never saw us. The group stopped and looked around. My husband stood up pointing his gun at them. I snuck, in the dark and grass, around to the side of the house. There was one guy, in the group, that also had a pistol. He raised the pistol towards my husband. I jumped out of the shadows and grabbed the gun. The guy tried to hold onto it, but my element of surprise caught him off guard. After a moment of struggle I got the pistol away from him. My husband was upset that I had done this – taking the risk of the struggle. Now both my husband and I had pistols pointed at the group. The group claimed they were sorry, they thought the house was unoccupied. They had intended to go into the house.

Now they just marched back up the hill, through our fields, and got back into the vehicle. We saw the vehicle lights go away. I awoke to pee.

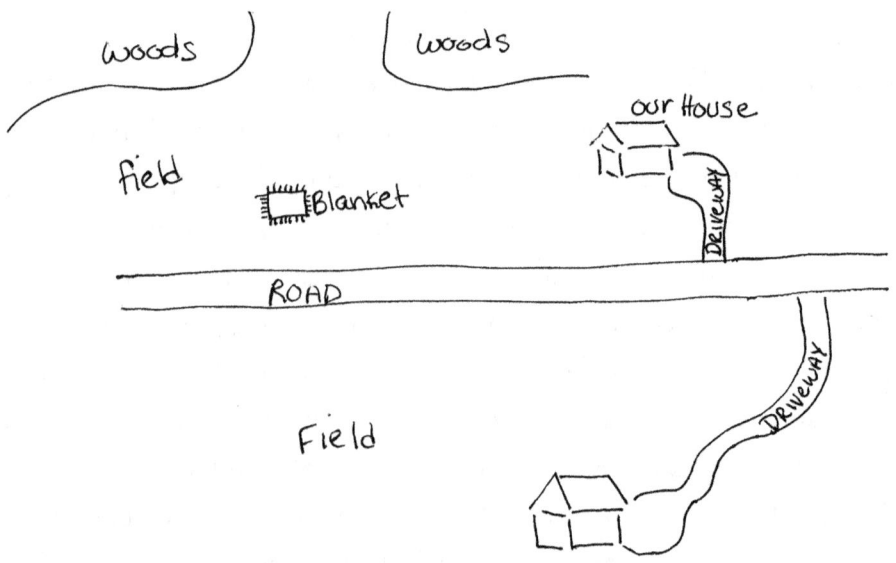

January 19

I was in an exercise class. Carolyn was there also. There was a lost and found area. It looked like a little shoe rack. On the bottom right were two pair of black shoes. Beside the shoes was a pair of black gloves. After class I looked over the lost and found. I noticed that all the stuff was ripped or torn. I threw it all away. Carolyn and I left the building. We walked a little ways through the town/city streets. I noticed a shop that was interesting. The shop owner was outside sorting beads on the sidewalk. I stopped being interested, I started sorting beads too. I had set my little black purse down within arm's reach. After a few moments I noticed my purse was gone. There was a teenage guy running down the street with my purse. I followed him. He went into a building. I peeked through a window and saw him go into a door that was made out of plywood. He came out, leaving the building without my purse. I went in the building, into the room with a plywood door. It was a tiny room. It was his shelter, and was only about 8' x 8' or less. I started looking for my purse. I searched his bed, I searched everywhere. At one point someone tried to come into the door. I held it closed. The plywood almost broke. I told the person, on the other side of the door, that a guy stole my purse. I was looking for it. He left the door alone and I continue to search for my purse. I awoke without finding my purse.

January 30

For some reason I was riding a horse in Mexico. (Most likely because Peggy Hill on "*King of the Hill* "took her class on a field trip to Mexico). My horse was a little unruly. There was a family walking on the same road, a woman and a little girl. My horse was headed right toward them. I was trying to make him stop. He finally did, but not before stomping on the little girls leg! Little girl's ankle was broken, her foot was turned out! I was responsible for her medical bills. My husband and I moved into a little house in a crowded neighborhood. The first night was terrible! There was so much noise we couldn't sleep. Some kids were terrorizing the neighborhood. We got up the next morning and left the house. I went to the house next door, and knocked on the door. I wanted to see if all the noise had come from them. The family was exhausted and thought we had been the noisy ones. We looked at the other houses next-door. There was a little window that was covered over. I removed the covering and looked inside. There was a large open room that looked like kids had partied in it. My husband went around the other side and went in to investigate. While he was in there, I looked around and found parts of what had originally covered the window. Originally the material was a heavy wood that locked on with a deadbolt. While my husband was in that room, I saw him fall down on his back. I asked him what happened; he said he had been shot! I ran around the building to another house behind that building. There I saw through a window a boy dressed as a cowboy with pistols. He was shooting out the window into the building my husband was in. I snuck up on the kid and grabbed him. I took him around the buildings and showed him to my husband and the neighbors across the way. I took the boy to jail. My husband recovered, it was a small caliber and he had been shot in the leg. The boy got out of jail and visited us, he had been rehabilitated. The boy was glad he had been caught, so he could straighten out. The neighborhood was quiet.

Another dream, later that night.

My husband and I went to a state park. We wanted to get from point A to B, so we took a log ride, down to where we wanted to be. I was in front, my husband was behind me. The ride had lots of stuff we had to duck down to avoid hitting. I was freaked out because there was lots of cobwebs hanging down. When we got to the bottom, of the ride, my arm was covered with cobwebs, from protecting my head. I awoke.

February 8 – Nap

I was on the phone with Aunt Nancy. I was trying to get an address for one of my cousins. I had to repeatedly ask her for the address. I couldn't hear her well due to my husband. He wouldn't shut up. He kept saying, "Bong bong bong bong bong bong". I was so mad! One of my cousins had married a guy from Australia, she had a new name. After many times of asking Aunt Nancy to repeat information, I gave up. I was so mad. When I got off the phone I was frustrated, from not getting the information I wanted. All this was due to my husband saying "Bong bong bong bong bong". I got up and frosted a chocolate cake. I took the cake and hit my husband in the head with it. I stormed out, pissed. I awoke exhausted, frustrated, pissed off and staggering. What an awful nap.

February 14

My husband and I bought a house. Cheryl and my son lived in it with us. There was a main part – old white porch on the front. The porch was more like an entry to the house – good place to put Christmas tree. A garage was attached to the house. The garage had no siding, just plywood. It was big enough for two cars but had one door in the center. There was another part of the house that seemed new. There were kitchens in both parts of the house. My husband, son and I stayed in the new part. In my son's room, up in a corner near the ceiling there was a group of wires coming out of the wall. Each wire was color-coded, rolled up and tied. My son kept complaining of noises coming from the wire area. These noises deeply disturbed him. One day he brought me into his room and told me about what was going on. I inspected the wire group. I thought the house was haunted! I called the realtor to come over. She stayed outside as we talked. I asked her, "What is up with the wires in the new portion of the house?" She finally told me that the house and burn and it could be haunted! I started to cry. I then asked her if we could divide the house in the middle of the garage and rented it out. She said, "No, you can't". I asked, "why not? There are two kitchens in the house. All we have to do is put a wall in the middle of the garage and change the garage door to regular doors". She again said, "No". I cried and cried. The thought of the fire struck me to my core. I did not want to be in the burned and repaired part of the house. I cried and cried. I awoke

February 17 – This dream is vague.

Hank T. was killed by some blue darts. I cried and cried.

Note: got a phone call upon waking – then hubby was yammering – I couldn't get to my dream journal quick enough for good recall. :-(

February 20

For some reason I was at WPI factory. WPI was bigger and much more expensive. I think I was cleaning offices. The president of the company was in a meeting with someone. I believe he was planning something bad concerning the company. I overheard parts the conversation. I was leaving the rooms and I saw Barbara. She was the only one I recognized. I started to talk to her and the president/CEO saw me. He grabbed me and dragged me outdoors around the corner. He started yelling and accusing me of telling Barbara about his evil plot against WPI. I slapped his face hard. I yelled back at him, "you ass! I have had quite a few grand mal seizures since I last worked here". He started to feel badly. I told him that my mind was Swiss cheese. The only person I could recognize was

Barbara. I was visiting with her and catching up. My conversation with her had nothing to do with WPI. I awoke.

February 21

I was in college, living in a dorm. Like many colleges, I had to walk to different buildings to get to my classes. The college was near a race track. As I was walking to another building, Jeff Gordon spoke to me. He asked me out! I was excited. I ran back to my room to change my clothes. He waited while I tried to figure out what shirt to wear. After trying on a few different shirts, wasting time, I asked my roommate if I could borrow a shirt. I met Jeff in a common area, downstairs in the dorm. He was patient. We got in his car and went for a ride. We visited and after a while I asked him, "how long has it been since you had been on a date"? He answered, "three years". I was shocked and asked him why. He replied that he is so busy with his racing circuit. But right now he had a day or two off before the race. We drove to the movies. I awoke.

February 24

I was working at a manufacturing plant. I don't know what we were manufacturing but it involved the use of screws. I worked second shift in production. There wasn't always much to do. Many of the employees just goofed off. I didn't like to goof off. So I used my time to come up with a better way to dispense the screws. Usually the screws were just taken from a bin. Many screws ended up on the floor. I had adapted a green Tonka toy truck some way to dispense the screws without them falling. One day a group of CEOs came in to look around. Our manager, Tim Allen (the comedian), was showing them around. I, at the time they were walking around, was on my hands and knees picking up screws on the floor. The suit said that I had some initiative. I stood up and said, "I have a way of stopping this wasting of time". They were interested in my idea. I took them to a closet where my invention was. I showed them how it worked, they liked it! I was given a promotion and was happy. While at lunch, a lovely buffet, Tim Allen came up to me and asked me to come to his office when I was done with my lunch. After lunch I went to his office. I peered into the office and saw him naked, admiring himself. I silently laughed at him. His penis was no bigger than an acorn. He was proud. LOL. I knocked on his door and entered. He wanted to have sex with me. I turned him down in the nicest way I could, without hurting his ego/feelings. I left his office and awoke.

February 28

I went home to Mom and Dad's to visit. While I was there I went for a walk. I walked by the farm my grandparents used own. I was horrified! When I got below the front field, I could see the farm. Someone had made it into something I couldn't describe. It was all lit up like a casino. So much had changed. The back of the barn, you can see from the road, had a couple of stalls with two horses in them. I think they were for racing. Everything else was lit up with neon colored lights. I walked up the hill for a closer look. I was again horrified! I started to cry. The place was like a casino or something. I went in and walked through every room I described, to myself, what each room used to be, when my grandparents owned it. I cried all the way through the house. At one point, I started kicking people out, fighting and hitting people. Fighting, crying, fighting, and crying. The people who were there were like squatters. I laid claim to it; the farm was my grandparent's. I fought everyone there, I kicked them all out. I cried. I awoke.

March 3

I won a contest of some sort. The prize was to go to a hotel with other winners and have a final contest. My friend, Suzy had won also. Suzie, I and many other women had to stay in one room. We used the hotel pool, most of the group was rowdy, and I was not. While at the pool, I spotted Johnny Depp! We made eye contact. He came over and spoke to me! Later, that evening, many of the girls left the room for a party, I did not. Johnny came by my room! We chatted for a while – he was seductive. I gave in to his seduction – this was Johnny Depp! We took off our clothes, even though I was married. He was so thin and wrinkly, I stared at him surprised at how wasted away his body was. He stared at me with my sagging breasts and ass- like stomach. Somehow we got past the surprising defects in our bodies. I reached out to touch his nipples. He said, that didn't do much for him. He turned his back to me and said, "Touch these; I get more delight from them". On his upper back were many moles that were protruding like nipples, there were seven of them. I was way turned off. Some of the girls started coming back to the room. I was glad that the tryst with Johnny was not going happen. We got dressed and he left. The next day, at checkout time, I was still in the room packing my things. My things were scattered in the mess of the room. A hotel employee came in and said that some of the women were going to be in trouble for their behavior – stealing and carrying on. I told the employee, "Don't look at me. I was not one of those misbehaving. The employee said, "Don't worry, we have them on videotape and will sort it out". I awoke.

March 11

My husband, daughter, son and I had to move out of the house. We moved into a communal barn situation. The accommodations were poor and we didn't have much. While there, my husband became friends with a woman. One day he came to me and told me he was leaving me to be with her. I was angry. I hit him in the face, but it was left-handed so there was not much power. The woman came in and tried to talk to me. I hit her as well, but again, left-hand. I wanted to pummel the both of them. I got in my vehicle and left. Kenny G. was with me. I got partway down the road and decided to turn around to get what I could my stuff. I returned for my pillow, blankets and anything else I could carry. I left again. I awoke taking household inventory in my head.

END OF VOLUME 4

VOLUME 5

March 12

I was at my great-grandfathers house for his birthday. There were so many people there. All of us were staying there for a few days. I mingled around. I found that I was not the closest relative there. I was one of the furthest removed relatives. I started to feel out of place. I was going to leave, I had an appointment in Alaska, and I needed to keep. I was driving there and it would take me days to get there. Someone tried to talk me out of driving to Alaska. I ended up staying an extra night, I was so tired. The next day I was frantic to get going. I was afraid I was going to miss my appointment. I woke.

March 13

I went to New York City with Suzy, Jill and my husband. We drove there in the Saab. I was wearing; pants, a shirt, rain boots to the knee and had an old umbrella that had no cloth on it, just a frame. We girls went to see a movie. I don't know what it was, but we enjoyed it greatly. The movie was not a in a theater, but a multipurpose place. The place was packed with people. When it was done, we dawdled behind the others. I asked the guy running the place how he had done that day. He got out a piece of paper and put down the day's receipts: $7000 something. He then subtracted the cost of buying the movie: $ 3000 something. So he did all right. The girls had gone to the car and I was dawdling. As I was leaving, I noticed a yoga class going on in a room near the exit. There was a glass wall to the right and I could see outside. I saw my husband, Sue and Jill in back seat of the car, visiting. I decided to walk around the block. I was swinging my umbrella, like a cane, enjoying my walk. I was in an alley. There was a pool that had rubber alligators in it. I touched one with the tip of my umbrella and it moved. It seemed real. I tried to touch another and it did the same. I moved along. There were rides on coin operated horses and other toy things on the way out of the alley. I think I was passing a toy store type business. It made me smile. I turned the corner, happily swinging my umbrella. At some point, I went into a building and had to go downstairs to get to the lower street. I was jumping down the stairs. I was enjoying myself. On the lower street there was some water running. This didn't bother me because I had my boots on. I waded in the water. I enjoyed this because of my boots. I was up on the main street again. The sidewalk was higher than the street. I walked along looking for stairway to get down to street. I needed to cross the road to get to the car. I found the stairs and started down them. There was a guy, a recognized, smoking a joint with some other people. I was surprised and happy to see him. He knew me, but didn't remember my name. He said, "J-name?" I replied, "No. I'm Bambi her mom". He said, "oh yeah" and passed me the joint. I motioned, No thank you to him. I noticed my umbrella had crapped out. I left the umbrella behind and crossed the street to the car. I awoke.

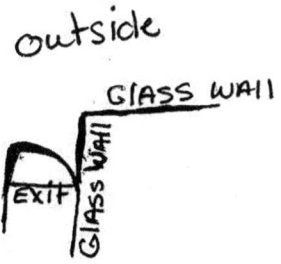

March 30

I lived in my grandparents house. I was with my first husband. There were many others living there with us. Becky, two other women, and a couple of other guys; one with dreadlocks and a weed smoker. The girls slept in one room, the guys slept in another room. There was a big hot tub in the living room. The building was practically falling down. The roof and the floor were bad. One day I felt my first husband was cheating on me with one of the girls. He denied it. Then I coaxed it out of him. He was having oral sex with one, not Becky. I slapped his face and told him and her to get out. We were all going to leave, the rent was over $3000 a month. The guy with the dreads was mad at me. He wiped his weed off the seat near the hot tub. Most of it went into the tub. I was going to say something but figured the filter will get it. A children's party was soon happening in the tub. I was in the tub, Puppa swam over to me. I went to the men's bedroom to talk to my first husband. There was a ceiling fan over his bed. I saw the fan start to wobble. The fan was wobbling so much it was coming out of the ceiling. I yelled to warn him. He ignored me. The fan was falling, it came all the way out of the ceiling! The fan just missed hitting him. The floor had great crevices in it, a foot deep. We were in great danger, living there. I awoke.

April 4

My husband, my first husband, mom, dad, granddaughter and myself, were at mom and dad's house. All of a sudden, many police cruisers came ripping into the driveway. We all stayed in the house.

We were scared of what was and what would happen. A backhoe showed up, the police started digging the Brook. Dad asked the cops what was going on. The man replied, "we know there's something hidden on this property will we find it, you're in trouble Mr.". Dad came back in the house and shrugged. We all watched out the window as the cops ripped up the whole property! The police made a huge plowed up mess. They found nothing. The police started plowing up the neighbor's property. Soon after starting on the neighbor's land, they stopped suddenly. They picked up something. The cop held it between his thumb and forefinger gently. He walked over to his cruiser with it. Dad went out to see what all the fuss was about. The item in the cops fingers was a little piece of metal/rock. The cop said, "good thing this wasn't on your property. We would have to run you in. Lucky for you your neighbor had it". The police took the neighbor away.

This may be a new dream. Not sure.

While at mom and dad's house, my first husband passed out. For some reason I thought it was best to take him to his home, instead of to the doctors. I took him, we got on a bus. The ride was very long; he was passed out most of the way. When we got within 20 miles of his house he awoke. He didn't know I was taking him home. He was disorientated as to his location. He was shocked at how long he'd been passed out. He didn't know why. I woke.

May 2

I was living in the city and dating Mel Gibson. He was handsome. There was something odd about him, that made me wonder. He was disabled, with a bum leg. He always showed up at places where I was. After the entertainment he would hobble in, kissed me, French, very passionately. The kiss seemed to be for show. His tongue would just spear my mouth and never touch anything inside my mouth. People would ou and aw and it seemed like a show. We would walk to his car, parked few blocks away. On the way we found a neatly set up crime scene. A baggie with cash in it, placed neatly with other items all laid out together. As we passed by Mel said, "Whoa stop- this is a crime scene". We called the police to tell them about it. Then we hobbled a short distance to his car. When we got to his car, he sat on the ground to rest, in front of his car. This was due to his disability. He lifted the hood and fished around in his pocket. There was a piece of plywood over the engine. He moved the plywood aside and found what he was looking for in his pocket, a screw. He took out a screwdriver and inserted the screw into the engine. The car started. He used the screw removal system to prevent car theft. We got into the car. There was a box of baggies in there. I began to suspect that Mel Gibson was the criminal. I woke.

May 28

For some reason I got pregnant by an older man. The older man moved me into his lovely old home. There, I found he already had a woman. The house was haunted. The woman was expecting me. I mostly stayed alone, roaming the house. one day very large man, with the bluest eyes, came in to do some construction. He was going to knock out a wall, behind the kitchen sink, to expand an area. I talked to him about the work. I didn't think it was a good idea. I felt it would anger the spirits in the house. The spirits had been relaxed and not bothersome up to now. I suspected, things would change if construction was done. The old man showed me a room that hadn't been used in many years. He said that room would be for the nursery. I didn't like it. I felt something would go on with the spirits of the house. Soon after that, the woman of the house told me that the old man wanted to start taking pictures of me. He was thinking of getting me my own place, with a studio for my artwork. I spoke to the old man and he wanted to show me his father. We went into a room that had been set up as a movie theater. He started a movie which shocked me. The movie was a slow-motion film of many naked people holding onto a pole. Those people were using their fingers on each other. The pole dance seemed like slow-motion due to a strobe light. A huge black man had his back to the camera; someone had a finger up his ass. The black man was getting off; his sperm was jetting out in slow-motion with the strobe effect. The older man said, "That's my father". I was appalled! I awoke.

June 19

I was at some lake. My husband and I had a rental unit. The buildings were all in a row, door after door with stairs going up to them. All the buildings were white with black hardware. Ours was somewhere near the end, but not quite. There was a smooth wooden thing, much like a turned over, propped up boat. I got on top of it, and slid down with my bare feet. It was very slippery. I kept doing this for a quite awhile. On my last slide down I got a piece of metal in my right foot. The piece of metal was sticking out the top of my foot, 8 to 10 inches long! A handsome guy came along and stopped to help me out. He withdrew the metal from the top of my foot. It was huge and had gone all the way through my foot! It didn't hurt much, once it was taken out. Maybe this was due to endorphins; maybe it was due to the cuteness of the guy. The man told me his name, but I didn't remember it. I thought Mike, but I think it was really Paul. We visited for awhile. I felt we had known each other somehow in the past. I introduced the man to my husband. My husband liked the man so we all hung out with each other for awhile. The man went home to another house on the lake. Each day I would see him and hang out with him, I felt he liked me. One day there were some games going on, out on the lake. The games were above and below the water. It snowed that day. The snow didn't affect the water temperature. I had a coat on but soon shed it I had a little hot wheel car with me. I put the little car it into a hole which ran a course dumping into the lake. I had to go underwater to get my little car. I dove down with my glasses on. I found the hole that the little car came out of, but there was no car there. I noticed neatly set rows of candy bars on the bottom of the lake. There were Hershey crunch bars, Take Five bars, Almond Joy, Nestlé chocolate, etc. I took a couple of candy bars and handed them up to my husband. I took a Take Five candy bar for myself. I then returned down to the hole, to look for my car. Now there was a pile of cars that had come out of the hole. I sorted through the cars and found mine. I came out of the water. I decided I needed to put on a bathing suit top, even though there was snow on the ground. I walked back to our rental unit, trying to decide which top to wear; my pink or blue one. I decided on the pink one. I didn't know which door was ours. I kept walking; I walked right by our door. Paul was sitting on our stoop. He called to me as I passed by. I turned around with a huge smile and awoke.

July 18

I was walking down the road, near where we lived. There was a stream going under the road. A man was fishing there. He caught one; it was a huge brook trout. The fish was so big! He laid it across both arms and had a hard time holding it up. It was the size of a German shepherd dog! It was a monster! I looked into the stream and there were many, more trout in the stream. I ran home to get my husband and granddaughter, so they could fish the stream. My granddaughter caught one! It was bigger than she was! I awoke.

July 26

I was somewhere, walking to a girl friend's house. On the way was a place that rescued animals. They mostly had horses. One day I walked by and there was a baby elephant. The dear thing was very small. He kept trying to go inside the building. For some reason the people didn't want it to go in the building. Whenever the little elephant would go inside a man would pick him up, by his back, and carry him outside again. The guy would grab him behind the neck and at his butt and lift him up. The baby elephant wasn't happy. My friend's house was on a big old farm. Her husband had just left her and the farm. There were no animals there, just stuff. The farm was a nice estate. When I arrived the front wall of the house was on fire! The fire was still small and could be put out. I ran into the house yelling about the fire. My friend said she knew and to let it go. She was going around the house, with other people, finding things that should be saved. I joined the group looking for things to save. The fire grew. I thought, many things should be saved, she did not. There was a group of glass sculptures on a shelf; I thought they should be saved. The glass was different colors of green, blue and white. The glass had been cut into curvy shapes. The front of each sculpture was smooth like sea glass. The backs were etched into fish and things. The woman had made these sculptures. She didn't want any of them! I took one and put it in my pocket. Very little did the woman want. I was a little freaked out about some of the things she was leaving behind. The fire department arrived. The woman went out to talk to them. She told them to let it burn, and they did. It was time to get out. The fire was much worse. My husband was with me now. We had to try and find a way out of the fire. It was like winding through a maze. We made it out. Finally I awoke.

August 12 – Nap

I have had this dream before (the houses are reoccurring)

I am at a house with my husband, Mom, Dad, Baker and my granddaughter. We lived at that house for a short while. It was a huge, strange house; it sprawled and had stairways everywhere. When I was at this house before: I owned a fawn Afghan hound. When we arrived, I noticed everything was the way we left it. No one had lived there since we had. I was showing, Mom, Dad and Baker around. Baker thought he'd like to live there. I went to show him a room I thought he would like. I left my granddaughter with Mom and Dad. I showed Baker the stairs leading to the back rooms. (illustration 17A) First I showed him the regular easy stairs. He loved the room those stairs led to. It was so big and had a kitchen set up. Next we went to the steep stairs. There was a big berm type thing going up the wall, beside those stairs. I stopped on the stairs to examine it. I pulled the top off and there was Easter candy in there, from years past. Half melted yellow marshmallow chicks, other half melted candies, a chocolate ball and some chocolate coins wrapped in foil. I took some thinking they would be okay to eat. Baker and I continued up the stairs to the room. He loved that one too; it also had a kitchen set up. We went back downstairs. You have to go through a slim bathroom that had a tub, to get to the other rooms. The tub was overflowing with water. I quickly pulled the drain plug and turned off the water. I continued through the bathroom, calling for my granddaughter. I found Mom and Dad huddled together crying. I asked what the problem was. They told me that they couldn't control my granddaughter. She kept running away from them and swearing repeatedly. I was mortified. I started to look for her. I couldn't find her anywhere. I went outside to look for her.

There was a man laying on a rock, relaxing. I asked him if he'd seen my granddaughter. He said, "No", and then started to cry. I asked him why he was crying. He told me that he didn't have long to live. He turned around and showed me a huge tumor on the back of his head. I started to cry for him. I touched his heart with my hand and walked away weeping. I went back inside still weeping. Mom and Dad were still crying. Mom and I went to look for Bella. We went into a room that had two beds and a glass ceiling. It was beautiful. Mom started feeling around near the bed located on the right of the room. There were prosthetic legs and crutches on the floor. Then I noticed someone was sleeping in the bed on the left of the room. I said, as quietly as possible, "Mom, this room is occupied". The man sleeping in the bed awoke and said, "It's okay". We explained why we were there then left him. I went to the other end of the house to look for my granddaughter; I called her name the whole way. I spotted her on some concrete stairs that lead to the first floor. (See illustration # 17B) I had never been down there before. My granddaughter looked at me, giggled and started down the stairs.

I was afraid she would fall and hurt herself on the concrete. I was flipping out! I was chasing her, calling her name. There were concrete troughs following alongside the stairs. I decided to slide down the troughs, to be quicker. It was so strange going this way and somehow my granddaughter was faster! She got over the catwalk beside the pools; where swimmers were competing in the pools. She made it to the other side! I had to skinny to the left of a swimmer on the catwalk. I said, "Excuse me". The swimmer moved aside for me. My granddaughter went back to the stairs. I had to excuse myself again to the same swimmer. This time she pushed me into the pool! Everyone was flabbergasted by this. I hit the bottom of the pool and shot up out of the water so fast. I was pissed, but it didn't have time to deal with her. I was after my granddaughter who was heading up the stairs. I started up the stairs after her. She came sliding down the trough. I was mortified; she was tumbling all the way. I thought she'd be killed by head trauma. I jumped into a trough and slid as fast as I could to try and catch up. When I got to the bottom she was not there. I awoke freaked out.

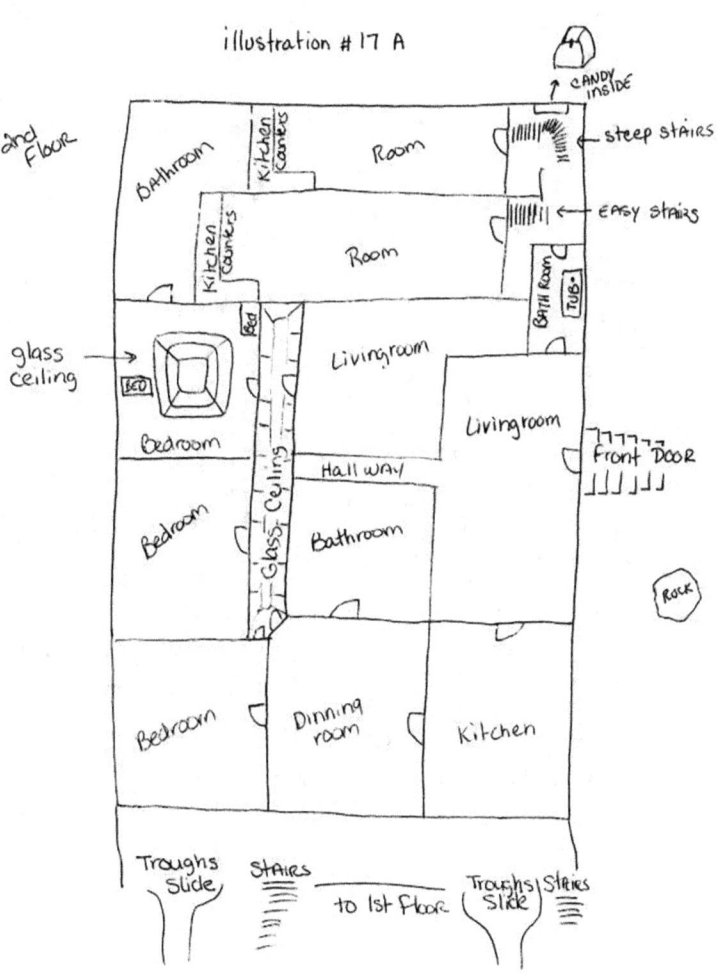

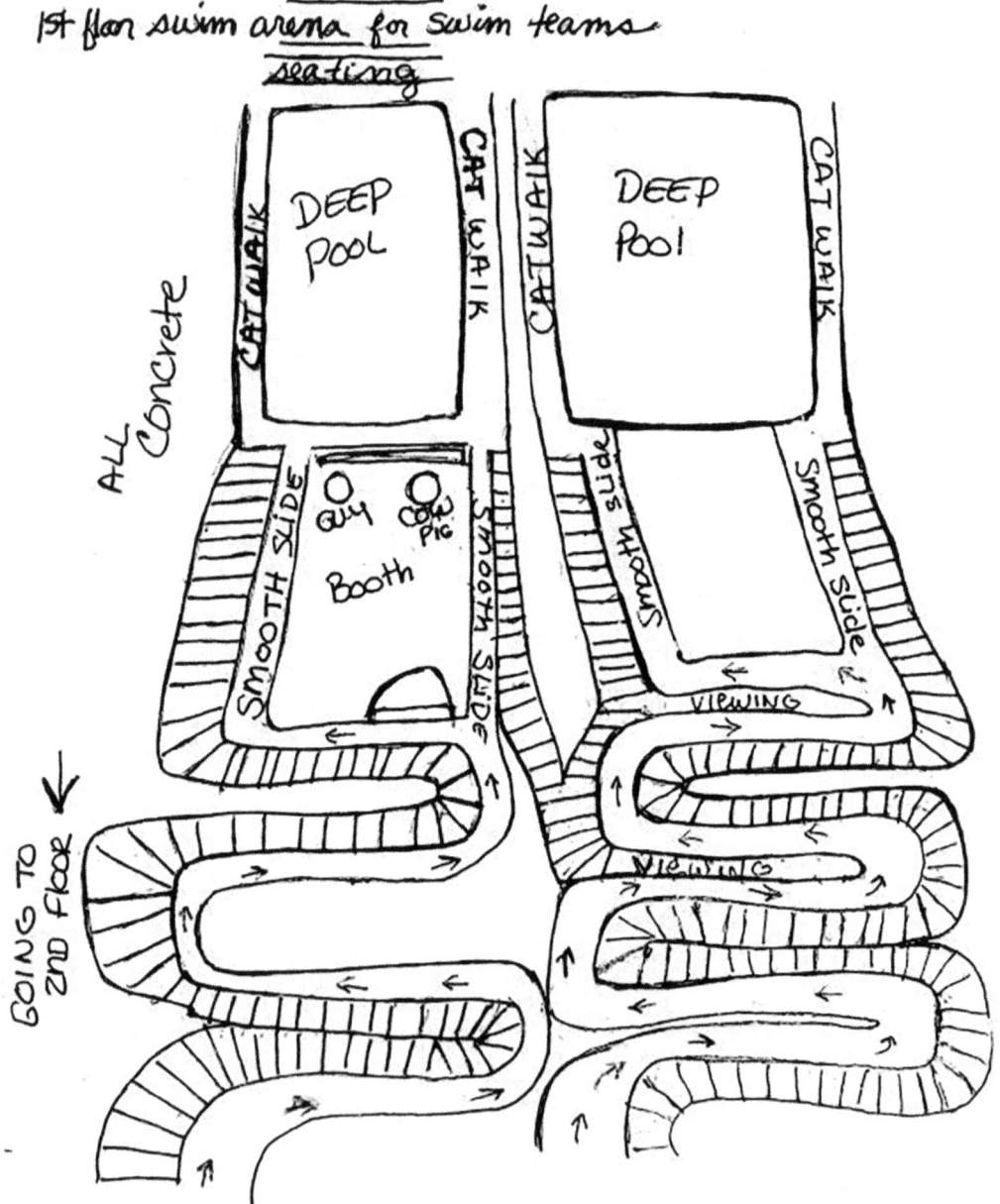

August 26

I saw Jill alive!! I don't recall if she came to the house or if I saw her elsewhere. I hugged her and didn't want to let her go. What had happened basically was she went underground. She'd had many surgeries; her belly was all scarred up. I was so happy. I was so mad. She had faked her death.

September 7

My husband and I bought a new house. It seemed like a condo that we weren't sharing with anyone else. There was a pond on the property, not a very big one. The bottom of the pond needed cleaning and it had a lot of turtles. My husband, granddaughter, brother, Dad and I were there. One night my hair stood straight up, the place was haunted. Out in the hallway I told dad about it, he huffed, not wanting to believe it. I said, "Watch this". Once again my hair stood straight up. I lifted my feet up, like I was kneeling, hovering in the air. I was at my regular height just with my legs curled up. The only reaction from dad and my brother was, "cool". I awoke.

September 15

I was going somewhere with Kenny G., we were on a church bus. We were sitting together talking. I got up, for some reason; my pants were covered in shit! Not just a little bit and nothing that could be covered with tying a shirt around my waist. The whole back of me was covered in shit! Most people on the bus see my pants. Kenny said, "What the hell"? I exclaimed, "I don't know". He said, "It must've been anal seepage". I replied, "This is a little extreme, why didn't I feel this"? We moved to the rear of the bus. People were staring at me and talking about me. As soon as the bus stopped, I got off It. People were very concerned about my shit. They started chasing me. I didn't know what their intentions were, but I wasn't going to stick around to find out. I started walking. The people followed, getting closer all the time. I ran and they ran after me. I took some kids bike and they still ran after me. I hid, down over an embankment by a river. The crowd passed me by. I was relieved, and washed off in the river. I awoke – clean – no anal seepage.

October 22

I shit out a vampire alien worm/snake. I bled a lot doing it. The creature looked like it was out of a movie, like Tremors. I did this over a concrete pit. It was small at the time of birth about 12 to 18 inches long. It, immediately was thrashing around looking for new food source. I tried to pick it up to examine it and it latched onto my finger and started sucking my blood. I had to rip it off and throw it back down into the pit. It kept trying to wiggle out of the pit and I would kick it back down. It became two creatures, then one ate the other. The one that fed became larger, like a constrictor snake. I don't recall how it ended.

My dream morphed:

I won a mini town truck at a raffle! The vehicle was so cool! It even had a trash container on the back that came with its own trash bags. You had to sit on top of it to drive, stagecoach style. The steering was rubber tubing attached to the front. You drove using the tubing like horses reins. It was pretty neat.

November 16

Carolyn, Wendy and I were in a city. I don't know where we were going or where we had been. Our trip involved luggage and we were driving a Jeep. We pulled over and parked. I walked over to a table, near where we parked. As I was walking by a drain grate my wallet fell into it. I told the girls my problem. They thought they could lift the grate to allow Wendy to hop down and get my wallet. I walked to the table and was refolding my clothes in my luggage. I looked over to my right and noticed a pair of chaps on the table. I rolled them up with my clothes. I started looking around and figured there was going to be a rummage sale the next day. A cop came by, he noticed me and not the girls, thank goodness. The cop took me into the station for a parking violation. At first, I was friendly and sociable to the cop because this was keeping him away from Carolyn and Wendy working at the grate. When I got to the station I asked the cop why he thought I was illegally parked. I stated that I was parked between the other cars and that there was a meter there.

My dream morphed:

My husband and I were dancing outdoors. There were many other people there. The guy, who played Jethro Bodine in the Beverly Hillbillies remake was the singer. I awoke.

THE END

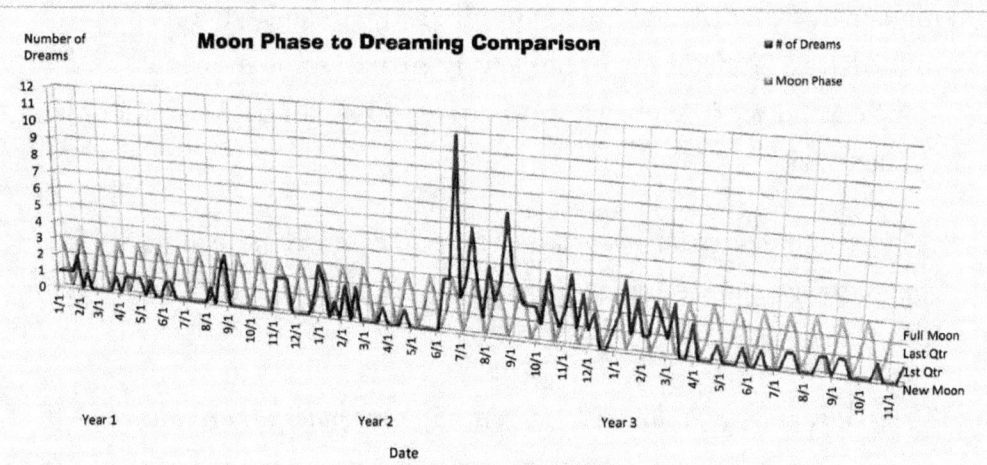

WARNING: IF YOU DON'T LIKE NIGHTMARES AND HORROR THEN DON'T READ THIS BOOK.

"Dream and Nightmares of a Menopausal Woman" is a collection of 157 extremely vivid dreams experienced over a 2 1/2 year period. Normally this would be nothing of great interest. But I am epileptic and one of the causes of my seizures is hormones. During the hormonal imbalance of menopause, I was basically allergic to myself! I never knew what was going to come at me each time I shut my eyes for sleep. Often not wanting to sleep due to the nightmares that plagued me. Not all of my dreams where nightmares. Some of my dreams were sexual, some hilarious, and some dotted with celebrities. A very unique read that also includes 19 illustrations.

"Unique and interesting opportunity to see the perspective of a woman going through quite a difficult menopause. Thankfully, menopause ends."
-Shelia Schwartz

" This adventure of a dream series journal, so wonderfully recalled, recorded and recounted in amazing detail, is a delightful and amusing experience. This book is a virtual 'smorgasbord' for dream and sleep researchers alike, who may find it an in depth challenge to interpret such. This book gives a whole new meaning to the words: pillow talk. Most delightful, Bambi Davis!" -Cheryl A. Hartwell

Bambi Davis lives in Newbury New Hampshire with her husband of 37 years. A bookkeeper and licensed tax preparer by day and multimedia artist by night. Bambi graduated from Hesser College with a degree in computer sciences. She is well known by local Native American communities for her knowledge of culture and ability to create traditional art. She shared these skills as a teacher and demonstrator at schools, craft fairs and living museums throughout New England. Her passion for expression now includes whimsical gardening, stonework, dancing and propagating the joy in every day.

www.ingramcontent.com/pod-product-compliance
Lightning Source LLC
LaVergne TN
LVHW020437070526
838199LV00063B/4763